TRANSFORMED

Scott & Sandy Boyd

T0151788

Carpenter's Son Publishing

Transformed

©2018 by Scott and Sandy Boyd

Published by Carpenter's Son Publishing, Franklin, Tennessee

Published in association with Larry Carpenter of Christian Book Services, LLC
www.christianbookservices.com

Edited by Christy Callahan

Cover and Interior Design by Suzanne Lawing

Printed in the United States of America

978-1-946889-45-4

A Warfare Manual is a lethal weapon in the hands of the holy.
—JEFF BALDWIN

We would like to thank Karen Tjossem and Diane Boyd who helped this book become a reality. This book would not have been possible without you.

CONTENTS

PART 1

My Testimony
By Sandy Boyd

Prologue

As I tried to look at my car radio clock, everything seemed blurred by tears, and my body shook with deep sobbing. Were they going to kill me? Who was that black hooded figure that stood at the foot of my bed? Would I ever be able to escape from this? Now they want my daughter! I looked at the razor blade, feeling it was the only way out.

1

Beginnings

Let's go back to the beginning. I was born in Pasadena, California, and raised in the small suburban town of Newbury Park. As part of a middle-class family, my life as the youngest of three daughters seemed normal and carefree. My sisters and I were two years apart in age, so naturally, the middle sister and I spent a lot of time together and shared a bedroom. It was what I call a love-hate relationship in that she was very bossy and picked on me quite a bit, yet we had fun times together as well. As we got older, my sister would spend most of her time at her friends' houses and eventually started running away and getting involved with drugs. She became very rebellious and disrespectful toward authority figures.

I was never close to my oldest sister, mainly due to the age difference between us. I only remember being awakened in the middle of the night hearing her and my dad yelling and screaming at each other on a regular basis. I didn't know why; I only knew that my family was changing and spiraling out of control. Something seemed to take a drastic turn for the worst around this time in my life, which I will explain later in this book.

My mother was a lunchroom lady in my early years at elementary school, and my dad was in scrap metal and owned a small refining business of precious metals. He would frequently bring home old jewelry and coins that my sisters and I were made to sort through. We had to separate the pure metal from the silver plated. My dad was very strict in that we had to ask his permission to do anything. For example, we had to ask if we could be excused from the dinner table. We had to eat everything set before us. If we didn't, we would sit there for hours until bedtime. If we still didn't finish, we would have to eat it the next day. If we reached over the dinner table to get something, my dad would smack our hands with a knife. We were to ask for it to be passed to us instead of reaching for it. When we would go out in a public place as a family, we, as the children, were to always walk behind our parents and would be punished if we would walk beside or in front of them. My dad always made my sisters and I massage his back, legs, and feet in the evening while he was watching TV. I don't ever remember my mother having a say in any of this; she always remained silent.

I played soccer as a child and participated in cheerleading as well. My real passion, however, was a love for horses. I always wanted a horse, as long as I could remember, and would cry whenever I saw a horse because I wanted one so badly.

I was very close to my grandmother on my father's side. I would spend the night at her house frequently. She lived right across the street from the school I attended. I used to dress up in her clothes and dance for her. I loved that because she was so attentive and would applaud after my performance. She also allowed me to play a waitress in the morning when I woke up. I would take her order for bacon and eggs and drink coffee with her. Every year she would make my cheerleading outfits by hand and would always make beautiful Easter dresses for my sisters and me as well. I truly loved spending time with my grandmother.

I was not nearly as close to my other grandparents on my mother's side. In fact, the only time I ever saw them was on holidays. They were both professionals working in the education system for a university in Sacramento. My grandmother was an English professor, and my grandfather was a science professor and actually studied under Albert Einstein at some point in his life. They traveled the world several times and were fascinated with different religious customs in other parts of the world. They would always bring us girls small gifts from each country they would explore. When they would visit us, I remember my grandmother always wore dark glasses which was an odd habit I thought. In fact, to this day, I never remember her without her dark glasses. She would continuously chain smoke and drink wine.

I grew up as a child in the late sixties, and my parents had a lot of parties. Our parents would leave us girls at home while they went across the street to participate in séances and drugs. I recall my mother telling me as a teenager that her mom and dad would have these types of parties while she was growing up. My mother's parents also frequented nudist camps, which they later owned. Sometimes when we would come home from school, we wouldn't be able to find mom anywhere. One time, my oldest sister finally found her passed out in the back of the station wagon all strung out on tranquilizers. I believe she was trying to cope with all the hell that was going on in our home. I will talk more about that in a moment.

SOMETHING BEGAN CHANGING

My dad seemed to always be at "the building" which is what he called his place of employment. He came home one evening after going to an estate sale of an acquaintance he knew whose wife had recently passed away. He bought an old antique corner hutch, which the old man said was his wife's favorite piece of furniture. He went on to explain that his wife had said before her death, that her spirit would always be present in that hutch after she was gone. This was very creepy to me, but my family found that fascinating.

Shortly after that, my mother's parents came to visit us and brought my sisters and me some books about witchcraft and how to perform incantations to cast spells. We were so excited to see if the spells would actually work or not. We learned to perform séances (summoning the spirits of those who had died). We would all be sitting in the living room as a family watching television and would hear odd noises coming from the new corner hutch. The noises were sounds of thumping and eerie creeks. There were also doors that opened and closed without anyone being near them. My parents immediately attributed these strange new noises to Mrs. Coral, the wife of the man we bought the hutch from. My parents went on to tell us girls that Mrs. Coral was there to protect us and befriend us. Unfortunately, this was a normal way of thinking in our family. This, along with the books given to us by our grandparents, seemed to mark the beginning of significant change in my life.

As time went on, we became comfortable with our newfound "friend," Mrs. Coral. We began regularly practicing witchcraft and having séances with our school friends in our garage. One time I remember casting a love spell on a boy I liked in the fourth grade. To my surprise, it worked! This was the first spell, among many, that I would perform. I felt a little silly waiting until the full moon at midnight to perform the ritual requiring me to run around my property naked reciting a series of chants.

My sisters and I would sit down beside Mrs. Coral's corner hutch and put our hands underneath it. We would then proceed to ask a series of yes or no questions. We used this hutch as a source of divination much like a Ouija board. We would ask things such as, will we get married or have a lot of money? We would feel a cool breeze from underneath and hear one thump to indicate if the answer was no and two if the answer was yes. Later, this experience would lead us into actually playing with a Ouija board and going deeper into the occult.

LESSON TAUGHT BY MY FAMILY

I remember one night while our family was sleeping, I woke up to the sound of crashing dishes. I ran to the kitchen to see the curtains on fire and dishes flying out of the cupboards hitting up against the wall. There was no one in the kitchen, and it was strange seeing this paranormal activity so blatantly displayed. I immediately ran to my parents' bedroom, where they were already on their way to see what the commotion was all about. Upon entering the kitchen, the dishes stopped flying through the air, and the fire was quickly put out. My parents had reassured me that Mrs. Coral was protecting our family by waking us up to the crashing of dishes to let us know there was a fire in the house. This Coral spirit was welcomed by our family as a benevolent spirit guide. Little did I know that this spirit would become my personal spirit guide and lead me into a lot of pain in my life. I don't remember if my sisters were there or not, and no one could explain how the fire started to begin with. I felt very relieved to have such protection around us. I would later find out how wrong I was.

My sister, with whom I shared a room, was beginning to wake up during the night with nightmares, which increasingly became worse over time. She was telling my mother that the nightmares she was experiencing always had to do with herself. She would wake up from these nightmares seeing herself standing over herself staring at her own body. This is what is known in the occult world as astral travel. I also astral-traveled without my consent quite a bit. Well, of course, at the time I thought my sister was crazy! My mother encouraged her by telling her that she had special gifts and that her grandmother (on my mother's side) was also blessed with these so-called "gifts" to see into the future and to have clairvoyant abilities. Now, I thought, *Wow! My mother and sister are both crazy!* Then one night I saw it for myself. I awoke as my sister was coming back into the bedroom after using the restroom. I watched her walk back to her bed. Later I heard her freak out and cry hysterically. As I sat up, I saw her looking down at herself lying in bed! I saw for myself that what she was experiencing was real, and we all accepted and embraced the explanation our mother told us.

THE DARKNESS THICKENS

From this point on in the story, when I refer to my grandmother, it will be my mother's mom to avoid any confusion.

My grandmother came to visit and brought me a beautiful sterling silver ring with a large onyx stone in it. I loved that ring! I never took it off my finger, even at bedtime. Within a week of wearing that ring, I experienced a frightening dream for three consecutive nights. In the dream, I lived in this dark valley where every night all the people who lived there had to be indoors before sunset. When it got dark outside, there was this strange thick fog that would descend and fill the valley. The fog would move from house to house and seek out anyone who was not hidden inside. If someone were exposed, the fog would consume them, and they would cease to exist. For the first two nights, I would run into a house and hide under a table until the horrible fog would lift. Then I would be safe. The third night I had the dream, everything happened exactly as the first two nights prior, except in this dream, I was hiding under the table, and I heard a very loud roaring hovering above my house. I was terrified and tried not to make a sound. Suddenly, the roof was ripped off, and the table I was hiding under was torn to pieces. As I huddled there, exposed, with no protection, I was snatched up into the dense fog. Then I woke up screaming. This dream seemed so real to me, and served as a pivotal point in the direction my life would take for the next 20 years. The seeds carefully planted in my life up to this point were about to take root and start growing.

THE TURNING POINT

I developed an unhealthy fascination with witchcraft, and it seemed that the more I studied and practiced the dark arts, the more my spiritual senses began to increase. My parents were fine with this and encouraged it, so I felt it was safe. My dad started to insist that I go with him to his building while he caught up on some work. This became his demand on a regular basis. One evening while there, he introduced me to marijuana. We would just smoke weed, sit, and talk. I was in the fifth grade getting high with my dad! I was too young to realize how weird this was. After a few times of doing this, I was excited to go. This led to harder drugs, and my father began touching me inappropriately.

At first, I resisted, but he would threaten me that he would deny me access to the drugs or other things I wanted. This behavior escalated to the point of taking nude pictures of me. He would soon start bringing pills into the equation. I became addicted to the pills and got to where I couldn't function when I was on them. I felt I needed them to get through the time I was alone with him. He told me that I could ask him for anything, and he would give it to me. He was the only one I was to ask. He set up this scenario to completely control my life. Because I was a child, I was vulnerable to this tactic. Unfortunately, because of my addiction, the powers of witchcraft, and his connections, he even controlled me into adulthood.

After losing my virginity to my own dad, I felt like this type of behavior was expected and started to sleep around with several boys. I thought, *Hey, if my dad is okay with it, what could be so wrong with it?* I decided to run away with a young man when I was in the sixth grade. He was nineteen years old and said he loved me, so I left home after leaving my mother a note telling her about what my dad was making me do. I thought I could get her attention and things would change, if only she knew what was happening. When I was supposed to meet my nineteen-year-old boyfriend, he never showed up to pick me up at our arranged meeting place. I called my mom to come and pick me up. I felt so scared and alone out there by myself. I needed my mom to protect me. My mom refused to believe that my dad would do such things, and I got in trouble for running away. After my mom talked to my dad, he admitted to having tried to touch me but said that was the extent of it. He didn't think anything was wrong with it, and apparently neither did my mom, because she chose to stay with him. That was the end of that. Life went on as usual. Nothing changed. I was convinced that my mom would not believe me if I continued to make any more accusations against my dad.

By this time in our lives, my oldest sister was gone most of the time. When she was home, the fighting escalated into the night hours. My middle sister continued to get in trouble a lot and was into street drugs. She would frequently run away and was very rebellious.

COMING INTO MONEY

In seventh grade, we moved to another, more extravagant part of the city. I realized that my sister I shared a room with didn't move with us. My parents just told me to get in the car. We had to visit her. I had no idea what was going on at that point. We drove into the parking lot of a psychiatric hospital. My dad told me that my sister was going to be there for a while. As we entered the door, I was so confused. I thought, *Why is my sister here in this place?* When I saw her, I cried. She didn't know who we were. The doctors had diagnosed her with Bipolar Disorder, and they had performed some electric shock treatments on her. She was out of control, so I was told. So this was the way my parents dealt with my sister as a troubled teen. It terrified me even more as to what my father was capable of doing.

When we moved, my dad bought me a horse and pretty much everything else I wanted. Not without a price, of course. He had an outside bedroom built for me. It had its own entrance so no one could monitor who or when people would come and go. He also had a hidden video camera installed, as I was highly encouraged to have my boyfriends come and stay the night. I didn't realize at the time that these sexual encounters with my father were increasingly becoming more satanic and ritual based.

My dad started to bring various antique artifacts into the family, and he began living as though he had come into a lot of money. Where did this money come from? Just as he was getting deeper into the satanic, wealth was increasing out of nowhere. He began driving expensive cars and living luxuriously. I recall one antique in particular. It was a satanic statue that stood about three and a half feet tall. The lower half was shaped like a horse, and the top half was a man holding a nude woman in his arms. This statue represents what my father became spiritually consumed with. It was a satyr spirit he had welcomed into his life. My dad's behavior was so strange. It became as though he was obsessed with this statue. He would sleep at night with it right beside his bed and would take it places with him when he would leave home. One evening while I was rubbing his back, I noticed three marks/scars etched on the back of his neck just under his hairline. I had never seen them before, so I asked him what they were. He immediately jumped up and, with great force, pushed me backward and started yelling at me to mind my own business, then sent me out of the room. Wow! I'd never seen him act like that before. He had such rage in his eyes. It scared me. Little did I realize at the time, he had truly sold his soul to satan.

Shortly after that incident, my dad introduced me to cocaine and a variety of new pills. Over the course of a few months, I became addicted. He gave me free access to the drugs at any time.

My sister had been in the psychiatric hospital for over two years by now and was ready to be released. I was starting my first year of high school. At this time, my parents had bought a huge house in Washington State and were preparing to move the family there. My oldest sister decided to move out and stay back in California. She wanted to finish school with her friends. The plan was for my dad to commute weekly and still maintain his business in California. We adapted quickly to our new location. My sister was doing much better and had a boyfriend that she spent most of her time with and later married.

I, on the other hand, was the only daughter still at home. Every week, when my dad would come home, he would quietly enter my bedroom in the middle of the night while I was asleep. I would awake with him on top of me chanting in a shallow unfamiliar voice. I would wake up and sense supernatural beings flooding into my room and what felt like hands touching me all over. I thought it was a dream that I couldn't wake up from. I was paralyzed, and all I could do to escape what was happening was to close my eyes and imagine a beautiful huge field of flowers (like in the movie *The Wizard of Oz*) that I would escape into. This imaginary place was my safe haven that I could run to. I felt I could be free there to dance, play, and feel peace. At this time I learned to mentally disassociate from all the darkness around me. Although I was familiar with the supernatural world I had learned about up to this point in my life; this experience was on an unfamiliar heightened level of evil and power I was not accustomed to. I felt pure evil in my room that night, and unfortunately, the rituals became more intensely demonic throughout my teenage years. What had my father gotten into spiritually?

I was expected to willingly endure this abuse in order to maintain my drug addiction. This was my father's plan all along. I was constantly told by my dad that I was useless to anyone else except him, and that he would always provide for me in every aspect of life. He went on to tell me that I would never be able to escape this hidden occult life. He told me this was my purpose for existence.

I was constantly in trouble at school. My social life consisted of a part-time boyfriend (whom my mom encouraged me to marry), parties, and getting so wasted that I would wake up in strange places, not knowing how I got there, and with strange people I didn't remember having had sexual relations with, both male and female. I didn't realize that my assignment was, through sex, to be used by satan to release into people's lives the evil that had been released in mine. Sex is a very effective tool of satan to release great evil into people's lives. I grieve now knowing how many lives were impacted by this. That is why the Bible teaches sexual purity.

I recall my dad giving me an abundance of reds (pills). I took them to school and was selling them to my friends. I had taken two of them myself before school. While sitting in math class, my teacher knew I was on something. I couldn't even write my own name on the paper. When I realized she was watching me, I thought, *I will just act like I was erasing something.* In doing that, I erased so hard that the paper tore in half. She immediately asked me to get up and go to the office. As I stood up, I was tripping and stumbling all the way. However, I did remember still having the pills in my pocket. So I quickly threw them into the bushes before entering the office. As I sat in the principal's office, he was asking me where I got the pills and how many people I gave them to. Well, I wasn't about to tell them that my dad gave them to me. I was so scared of the trouble I would be in if I were to tell him the truth. As a result, I was suspended for a few days.

During my senior year of high school, my parents decided to get a divorce but had an agreement that my dad would still continue to support us financially. He would have free access to come and go as he pleased. My mom had a boyfriend who had moved in with us, which seemed totally fine with my dad.

After having an argument with my boyfriend about not wanting to marry him, it quickly turned into a very violent physical altercation in the front yard of my house. As he continued to pull my hair, throwing me to the ground and hitting me in the face, I struggled to make my way to the front door, screaming for my mom to help me. I saw her running to the door and thought she would open it for me, but instead, she locked the door. She began yelling at me that I deserved everything that was happening. As I lay there bloody on the front porch, my boyfriend finally left, and I heard the door unlock. Holding on to the door knob for support, I pulled myself up and made my way into the house, all while trying to get to a phone so I could call the police. Suddenly, I felt someone grab my hair and pull my head back forcefully to the floor. My mother's boyfriend sat on top of me, holding my head with both hands, then proceeded to slam my head onto the floor as he repeatedly told me I didn't have permission to use the phone.

THE RESULT OF FAMILY BETRAYAL

I felt so lost, abandoned, and broken. I just hoped somehow I could find someone to take me away from all this. I never graduated from high school. In fact, I never went back home after that horrible life-changing experience. I ran away and found myself in a different city about five hours away. I stayed wherever I could and with whomever I could. Sometimes I would stay on the streets, cold and hungry, while other times I would have a place to sleep only in return for sex. I refused to have any contact with my family until I could no longer support my drug habit and was forced to reconnect with my dad. He decided to fly me out to California and set me up with various acquaintances to perform sexual acts for money. By this point, I had developed a deep-seated hatred toward men. I thought they would all only hurt and use me. As a result, I had built an unseen wall around myself that no one could penetrate. I was determined to never submit myself willingly to anyone. But in reality, I couldn't live without the direction of someone telling me what to do. No one had ever taught me how to make decisions for myself.

As I continued my search for someone to show me love, I was desperate to be in control of my own life. I met a man and dated him for a couple of weeks. When his brother, who was quite a bit older than me, showed an interest in me, we got married quickly. He didn't know a thing about my life or where I had come from. I continued to go out at night and do what I had to for drugs. My husband was an alcoholic, and we would fight a lot and do the party scene with his mother and her husband. My dad would somehow always find out where I lived and my phone number, and he would call me randomly or just show up to entice me with drugs.

A VICIOUS CYCLE

I was never strong enough to resist the temptation of the drugs, which resulted in the vicious cycle continuing to control my life.

After four years of marriage, I became pregnant with my son. It was the happiest day of my life. I finally felt that I had a purpose and someone to live for. I believed this could be someone I could love without stipulations or demands, and someone who would unconditionally love me back. Our little family moved to Texas, where my husband's dad was living at the time. We moved in with him and his wife. Unfortunately, I quickly became aware that my father-in-law, who was a former evangelist, had turned his back on God and was also struggling with alcoholism. He and his wife would fight a lot, and we all lived in a constant state of discord until my husband and I moved into our own place.

I would spend most of my time with my little boy. He was my whole world and brought me such joy. As dysfunctional as it sounds, my family at this time was so much more than I ever had growing up, even with all the drugs, alcohol, and fighting.

My dad again tracked me down and randomly showed up on my front porch one day. He was furious, telling me that he warned me about trying to disconnect from him. He then offered me drugs, which I accepted because an addict never turns down free drugs. He knew exactly how to manipulate me. After all, he was the one that had manipulated my entire life. What he did to me as a child was to condition me to submit to his control.

I was so angry with myself. I hated who I had become. After that incident, I came to a point where I didn't care anymore about my so-called quaint little family. My dad was back on the scene in control of my life again. My husband had filed for divorce and threatened to gain full custody of our son. He moved in with his family, and I took my son and drove off in my car, having no idea where or how I planned to provide for us.

I quickly realized I had to cover up my addiction and living conditions. I was living in my car. I finally found a part-time job at a convenience store. I had to somehow prove to the court that I could provide for my son. He alone was the only thing that gave me strength to change the way things were. My dad agreed to help with a lawyer if I would meet him at a hotel and stay with him for a couple of days to "pay" for his help. For the first time in my life, I refused his proposition. I didn't want him to be in any part of my son's life. The only thing he had to say to that was, "You will be back."

Because I had no money, I represented myself in the fight to keep my son. I had pretty much lost the case before ever entering the court room. After all, what kind of mom was I? My father-in-law stood in agreement with my ex-husband, of course. He claimed that he would help to provide a stable living environment for the baby and his dad.

My mother also played a role in the case by claiming that I had always been unstable and incapable of raising my son. Defenseless against all the accusations brought about in the case, I lost all rights to my son. I was devastated. This was a crushing blow that felt as though my heart was ripped out of my chest. The *only* thing I ever felt true love for was my son. Now he was totally ripped out of my life without even visitation rights. I was ordered to pay child support, which started the process of my wages being garnished. During my son's whole life, I had to fight and beg my ex-husband to see my son on his terms. He seemed to enjoy hurting me and making this process almost impossible. So needless to say, no matter how hard I tried, I never was a part of my son's life.

Unfortunately, my dad was right. I had nowhere to go and no one to turn to. I went to the hotel where he was staying, and he paid the price for an apartment and for me to get started in beauty school. I was determined to get a good job to provide evidence that I could take care of my son someday. That was the goal anyway. I was doing pretty well in school. My dad would come periodically and demand payment for me to continue in school and provide a never-ending supply of drugs. I was a month away from graduating from beauty school and was so proud of this accomplishment. I arrived at my apartment one evening after school to find a lock on my door. I was confused as to what was going on, so I went to the manager, asking him why the lock was on the door.

It wasn't much, but everything I owned was in there. He replied that my dad had stopped payment on that month's check. Hysterically, I called my dad. I stated that I was so close to graduating from beauty school. I asked him why he would do this. He had told me that after graduation, I was to take my son and come to California. He had assured me that he would hide us underground from the authorities. "They will never find you," he said. He went on to say I would never have to worry about being away from my son again. He would take care of us. He had demanded that I kidnap my son! Was that really what was happening?

I just couldn't jeopardize the safety of my son to this monster. I knew what he was capable of, and I knew that it would never end for me or my son. Because I would not comply, I lost everything in that apartment. I also lost the dream of graduating from beauty school. Shortly after that, my car was repossessed. Once again, I had to live on the streets doing the only thing I knew to survive.

I had received word that my ex-husband was taking my son and moving to California with his mom, and I wouldn't see him again. I remember finding a ride out to where they were living to try to reason with my ex before he left the state. I arrived to find the gate was shut and locked.

I stood outside the car, screaming for my son. When my father-in-law came out and said that they had already left, I snapped and was out of control. I was trying to climb the gate while he was threatening me to get off his property. The person I was riding with forced me back into the car, and we drove away.

I couldn't bear the thought of never seeing my son again. I wanted the driver to go after my ex and son, but when he drove in the opposite direction, I jumped out of the car, which was going 50 mph. I tried running after them. My heart was to find a way back to the California-Washington area to be near my son, even if it meant taking orders from his dad.

I lost my job at the convenience store because I didn't have a car to get there. I thought that I could fix my life without my dad's help. In reality, I just found other people like him to support my drug habit. After all, the price required of me was all the same anyway.

I found an abandoned house to live in. I was content with having a roof over my head and filthy carpet to sleep on. I met a man who lived up the street and bought me a mattress and blankets to put in the house. He contacted the landlord and paid my rent for a month. He turned me on to some new drugs (crank/speed). So the cycle continued. We got married shortly after we met and partied all hours of the night. He worked nights, so I would hang out with drug dealers and stay up for days at a time. I recall being up for three days straight, barricading myself in the house because I thought the police were stalking me. I literally thought they had my house surrounded. I didn't eat or sleep, and I became sick and unhealthy.

I became pregnant with our daughter. After her birth, I finally convinced my husband to move to Washington State, where my sisters lived. In fact, we rented a house right next to my oldest sister and her husband, who had moved there a few years earlier from California. We would occasionally party with my sister, and it didn't take long for my husband and me to find the right drug dealers in the area for our supply. I would be out all hours of the night at bars and going home with strangers while my husband was at home with our daughter. Then I would return home to care for her while my husband went to work in the morning. My sister was angry with me because of my lifestyle and didn't have much to do with me at that time. Within a year, my husband and I divorced. I tried to stay in the house for a while, living on only the child support I received and food stamps. It would freeze in Washington in the winter time, and there were holes in the roof of the house. I had only a wood stove for heat but didn't have money for firewood. I would go next door and ask my sister for some wood to keep my daughter and I warm. She always refused. So I had to wait until dark and sneak over to the neighbor's house across the street and steal wood to keep warm.

I couldn't afford living there without a supplemental income. So I asked my friends, who were lesbians, to move in with me. Because we had all had a brief relationship together, they quickly agreed. But within six months, my roommates decided to move out of state, and I was left with the decision of where to go next.

SIGNS OF WHAT WAS TO COME

I lived about eight hours from where my son and his dad were living, and I drove to see him as much as possible. This required his father's permission of course. I would often ask my middle sister to come with me. We would drive along the coast and usually stay the weekend. One time in particular, I recall riding in the passenger's seat while my sister drove. Something strange caught my attention. While driving down a curving slope, I was looking out at the beautiful vast ocean. There was a small area where people could pull off the main highway to enjoy the view. No one was there when we passed by, but I thought I saw a sheep. Yes, that's right, one lone sheep wondering around by the ocean. I asked myself, *Did I really just see one sheep by himself? I thought sheep stayed together in a flock.* This didn't make sense in my mind because on one side of the highway had been the wide-open sea for miles, and on the other side of us was only steep, rugged mountain terrain and rocks. I was determined to go back and make sure that what I thought I saw was really what I saw.

Asking my sister to turn around quickly, we drove slowly past the lookout point, and there it was. I couldn't believe my eyes! We pulled over to get a closer look. He just stared at us. So I thought, *I'll just try to get closer and maybe I can pet him.* As I walked closer to him, I noticed he was hurt and limping on one foot. I felt such compassion for him. *He will never survive out here without help.* As I walked closer to him, he backed up to keep his distance. This went on until he reached the edge of the cliff overlooking the ocean. This sheep would rather fall off this cliff to his death than to let me get close enough to help him. I felt sad for the sheep, but I didn't want to be directly responsible for his death. I returned to the car, and we drove off. This experience would play a significant role in my life as you will see. This wounded lamb was a sign of what was to come.

My middle sister was divorced now and living on her own. She invited my daughter and I to stay with her. I had a part-time job and received welfare, which took care of some expenses as well. It was very strange after moving in with her. We would get high together and experience supernatural encounters on a whole new level than when we were kids. There seemed to be a darker power at work in our lives now. It was as though a thick, heavy darkness had settled over us. I guess the best way to describe it is that the powers she possessed, combined with mine, were unprecedented compared to any other time in our lives. We were aware of the unseen forces at work, but we didn't know how to control them. I had an on-and-off boyfriend who was one of the biggest drug dealers in the Portland area at the time. I met him while working at a bar as a stripper. I felt in total control of who I would have sex with and who I wouldn't. I was a teaser for sure. I would let men get close to me, just to hurt them for what other men had done to me. The behavior was my subconscious way of getting revenge for the hurt men had inflicted on me in the past.

As I was getting ready for work one night, I watched the news on the television. They were reporting about a woman who had been murdered and her body thrown in a dumpster behind the same bar where I worked. She was a coworker of mine who had left work shortly after I did the night before. I was terrified. This really was hitting home. I thought, *This could have been me.* Needless to say, I didn't hesitate to quit that job.

My daughter was growing up fast, and she was talking a lot. I wanted to keep a record of her first words, so I purchased a small tape recorder. After recording her talking gibberish, I played back the recording so I could listen to it. I will try my best to describe what I heard. It definitely was not of this world as we know it. I heard what sounded like horrible screaming and people being tortured and put in bondage by what sounded like chains being thrashed about and locked into place. There were loud roaring noises and babies crying. Fear gripped me, and I couldn't move. I was so terrified at what I just heard. My daughter's words were not on the recording at all.

After pulling myself together, my sister arrived home. She knew something was wrong with me just by my facial expression. I had a hard time explaining what I had heard, so I played the recording for her. She literally freaked out, and with terror in her eyes she screamed at me, "What have you brought into this house?" Pushing me out the door, she demanded that I get that thing out of her house.

I didn't know what to do with it, so I proceeded to my drug dealer's house. I told her what happened and let her listen to the cassette. Much to my surprise, she started to laugh. "That's so cool," she said. "I want to put that on my answering machine." I had no problem with that as I just wanted to get rid of it any way I could.

Relieved, I went back home to find that my sister wasn't there. While I was getting ready to go out that evening, I was putting my makeup on and listening to AC/DC on the radio. I was singing along and all of a sudden, the music started to fade, and all I could hear was the horrifying sounds that were on the tape I had recorded two hours earlier. How could it be! I thought, *It's following me!* I had to go destroy that tape, or it would never stop. I ran to my car, and I drove over to my dealer's house. I stormed through the front door, screaming that I needed to get that tape back. Within her bedroom, my dealer lay on the floor with her eyes rolled back in her head, blood coming from her mouth, and the same sounds on the tape coming from her vocal chords. I immediately grabbed the tape from her machine and took a hammer and destroyed the tape.

She finally became conscious and had no recollection of what happened after she put the tape into her answering machine. Lying in bed that night, I was trying to make sense of the intensity of demonic activity flooding in and around my life. I didn't have any idea why this was happening or how to stop it.

I fell off to sleep, only to be awakened by something bumping my bed. I sat up, and at the end of my bed stood a dark hooded figure about seven feet tall. Thinking it was a dream, I lay back down. It happened again, and this time I heard a voice coming from the figure. He said to me, "It's time," over and over. Finally, I asked, "It's time for what?"

He said, "It's time *now* to pass on to your daughter what your grandmother has passed on to you." Then the figure disappeared.

What? I didn't understand at first. I pondered that statement through the entire night. What exactly was I to do? The next day, while talking to my mother, she told me that my grandmother had passed away a short time ago. It hit me like a ton of bricks. I heard the words in my mind: *It's time.* I somehow realized the supernatural abilities passed on to me from my grandmother were meant to be passed on to my descendants. This explained the increase in darkness and the paranormal activity.

I couldn't believe it! At twenty-nine years old, I realized that there was no way I had the power to change my life or the life of my child. This was totally out of my control. I knew in my heart that I could never fight against or escape these demonic forces.

At that moment I remembered what my dad had told me so many times growing up. He stated over and over that I would never be able to escape this life. Did he know all along? Was this truly his plan for us from the beginning? Was it my grandmother's intention to lead my sisters and I into this nightmare that would consume our lives? I believe that it was. They had given their lives to satan, and they had dedicated me as a child to satan. Where was my mom when all this was happening? Did she knowingly allow her little daughters to be the victims of this perverted, twisted game? Was she a victim herself? The damage was done. It went on to affect my life and that of my sisters. Unfortunately, our children have been very damaged as well. My parents were the very ones that were supposed to protect us. They were supposed to teach us to be loving, faithful wives to our husbands and how to lead our own children by example. They should have shown us how to live productive lives, and how to love others, because we had been properly loved.

So many questions arose in my heart. So much anger, hurt, feelings of abandonment, betrayal, and unforgiveness. What had we done that deserved so much pain that it would last a lifetime? Would we ever be able to break out of the walls of protection that we'd learned to build around ourselves and live happy, normal lives?

Feeling hopeless, I contemplated where my life and that of my daughter would go from that point. All hope was lost in my mind. The goal was to find a safe place for my daughter. I felt that my life was worth nothing, and I didn't know how to protect her from my family. I truthfully thought that my only option was to take my own life. I could leave my daughter at her babysitter's with a note in her backpack with specific instructions that my daughter was *not* to be put in the custody of my family members for any reason. I wanted her to have a chance to be raised in a loving home with loving parents whether it be in foster care or through adoption. I didn't care as long as it was away from my family!

AT A CROSSROADS

I proceeded to take her and drop her off at the sitter's house. Then I drove to a secluded field where I was prepared to end my life. Crying uncontrollably, I was so afraid but didn't see any other way. I took the razor blade in my left hand, intending to slit my right wrist. I leaned my seat back in a reclined position as my right arm fell beside me in between my seat and console. I was distracted by something I felt had fallen down between my seat and the console. I picked it up, and thought, "What is this?" What I held in my hand would *forever* change my life as I knew it.

In my hand, I held a small pocket-sized green Gideon Bible. Where had this come from? Your guess is as good as mine! I had not been associated with any Christians of any kind. As a matter of fact, I obtained the car through a drug deal a couple of years before. While wiping tears from my eyes, so I could investigate this little book further, I proceeded to skim through it.

I didn't understand anything, but turning to the back cover, I read through the prayer for sinners. I could totally relate to what the words on that page were conveying. I prayed that little prayer and asked Jesus to take complete control of my life that day in the front seat of my car. What I felt was amazing! I couldn't physically see someone in that car with me, but I truly felt such compassionate loving arms around me, engulfing every part of me from the inside out. I felt like I was being cuddled up and rocked back and forth. A peace engulfed me that I had never experienced before in my life. This peace filled my very being. Something big had just happened. In my entire life, I had never heard about Jesus. The only exposure to him I had was the movie *Jesus Christ Superstar*. That movie was certainly not the best portrayal of him, but I remember feeling drawn to that movie as a child.

Jesus met me right where I was that day. Now every intention satan had to destroy my life was going to be directly challenged. My life was now under the blood of my Lord and Savior who thought I was worth saving.

I may not have looked any different on the outside, but there was a significant change on the inside. My heart was changed, and all I wanted was more of Him. As I drove to pick up my little girl, I recited the sinner's prayer over and over. I held onto the fact that He promised me eternal life if I would surrender my life wholeheartedly to him.

I picked up my daughter, and we went home. I was excited about what had happened and what I felt on the inside. I had no idea how to react to this newfound relationship with Jesus, but one thing was for sure—I knew the sinner's prayer!

THE BATTLE WAS ON

About an hour after I laid my daughter down for bed, I heard her screaming. I quickly ran into her room. As I flipped the light on, I saw toys flying around the room and her ceiling fan spinning so fast I thought it would literally fall from the ceiling. It was like a spiritual whirlwind of rage had broken into this room. While I was trying to comprehend all that was happening around me, I saw my daughter standing up in her crib. Her arms were flailing about as she screamed, "Mommy, they're biting me!" I immediately ran to pick her up and saw actual bite marks on her arms. We were both terrified. Running into the living room, I held her tight. We huddled in the corner of the room, and I rocked her reciting the sinner's prayer all night long.

Morning came, and I thanked Jesus for keeping us safe. I found myself pondering the night's events. Then I remembered back to the incident of my childhood when Mrs. Coral caused the dishes in the kitchen to fly across the room to warn about the fire that mysteriously started (which she probably started in the first place). I knew this incident was different. There was pure evil in my daughter's room. There is no doubt these spirits intended to cause harm, not protection. My parents taught us they were good spirits. Yeah, right! They were pure evil and really hated us. They only wanted death and destruction for our lives. We were just too blind to see it. I struggled to make sense of it all.

When my sister returned home, I was so anxious to tell her about my experience with Jesus. I just knew she would accept him, and we would both start a new life. She was very distracted while I tried to talk to her. She just continued to insist that I make a drug run for her. I tried to tell her that I was giving up that life. I didn't want any more drugs. I had found someone worth giving it all up for—Jesus! She laughed at me. Then she became angry because I refused to get the drugs for her. She totally tuned me out after a time, so I turned to leave the room. I heard a scream behind me, and as I turned around toward her, she jumped on me. In a fit of rage, she started punching me. I was shocked at her violent outburst but, strangely enough, I felt the same peace come over me that I had felt in the front seat of my car the day I accepted Jesus. I didn't even fight back. Wow! I was not at all the same person I used to be. The old me would have fought back for sure. My sister proceeded to grab my hair and pull me out of her front door, telling me never to come back.

A BIZARRE VISION

I didn't know where to turn, so I called my drug dealer boyfriend. This time I didn't call for drugs, but out of desperation for a place to stay. While there, I experienced severe demonic phenomena. I was awakened by very loud heavy metal music. As I stepped into the living area to investigate, I saw my boyfriend high on drugs lying on the floor. I felt the ground around the whole house shake. Then I saw in the center of the room a huge hole open up as everything was beginning to be sucked underground. I was screaming and pulling him away from the hole. He finally got up and was able to run with me out of the house. We were in the middle of the yard as we watched in astonishment the house crumbling to the ground and being pulled under.

He started going back toward the house while saying that he needed to retrieve all of his music CDs. I was yelling at him to not go back into the house. I told him if he did go back in, he would never come back out. Ignoring me, he ran in. When I could no longer see him, the house was completely gone. I left and stayed with a friend that night. When I returned the next morning, everything seemed normal. I was not high on drugs at the time that I saw that vision. I literally saw this happening, and he saw it as well. I believe this was a glimpse into the spirit realm that God allowed me to see. It was as if, all around us, hell was opening up and trying to pull people into it. As with past experiences, all these things were taking place in the spiritual realm. For some reason, I believe God was allowing me to see in the spirit what the enemy had kept me from seeing all these years. The enemy of my soul was bent on my destruction.

Although my boyfriend convinced me to do some drugs with him and perform sexual favors for him—and I was still in bondage to cigarettes, drugs, and alcohol—I felt so sorry to the Lord for doing so. This was a miracle because I had no way of knowing this behavior was even wrong. My parents raised me in a way that this was normal. So why was I now feeling it was wrong? It was the Lord living in me! For the first time in my life, I felt repentant. Of course, I didn't know it at the time, but the beautiful Holy Spirit was teaching me to feel with the heart of God. How sad that I had wasted my entire life up to that point on worthless and evil things. At the same time, it was beautiful seeing that God was beginning to work in my life.

TIME FOR MAJOR CHANGE

After a week or so of staying with my boyfriend, things became unbearable in everything he expected of me and all the illegal activity occurring. I stayed secluded as much as possible. I started filling my mind with the Word of God. The scripture that stood out to me was Luke 15:7. This scripture talks about how all of heaven will rejoice at one sinner that comes to the Lord. I also read Psalm 23. This scripture spoke of the Lord being my Shepherd. I instantly thought of the experience I had with the sheep while driving along the coast. I saw myself as that lost sheep, wounded and alone, and Jesus came and found me on the verge of ending my life. There was no doubt in my mind this was a sign of what was to come. What a beautiful thought! At times, I would feel my heavenly Father come into the room and put His arms of comfort around me just like the first day I met him. I so desperately wanted to live for him but didn't know where to start. I was such a babe in Christ.

While praying one afternoon, I randomly had a thought enter my mind. I thought of Texas. *What? Who do I know in Texas?* I thought of my first husband's father. I remembered him as the one who hated me enough to be a part of taking my son away. He was the one who ordered me off his property and threatened to call the police. I didn't have the best memories of this man. After ten years, there was no way he would ever want to talk to me again. Then I recalled that he was the only person I knew who could tell me about being a Christian. After all, he used to be one.

After struggling with the idea, I called him. I was surprised when he didn't hang up on me. He listened quietly while I apologized for everything I had said and done. I informed him about all that was going on and my love for Jesus. I also explained how I was experiencing supernatural opposition and was confused as to why these spirits who once protected me were now trying to hurt me. I heard sympathy on the other end of the phone as he told me that he was so very sorry for the way things turned out with my son. He apologized for allowing himself to be part of that. He had rededicated his life to the Lord and recently started a church in his home.

He went on to explain how satan was not happy with my decision to serve the Lord, and that all these years the spirits at work in my life were from satan himself to keep me in bondage. I was utterly shocked at what he was saying, but I thought back to how the spiritual dynamics had changed over the course of my life. It was starting to make sense now.

Concerned for my safety and spiritual growth, my former father-in-law offered to buy plane tickets for my daughter and me to fly to Texas and stay with him and his wife. He explained the importance of being surrounded by godly people who could help in my spiritual growth process. He wanted to teach me how to fight this battle that I was now engaged in. I was hesitant at first because the reason I moved back to Washington was to be near my son and maintain some kind of relationship with him. I feared being so far away that he would not remember me as his mother who loved him very much. At the same time, I desperately needed to protect my daughter. The only way to do that was to completely remove myself from that geographic area for a time. I made the decision to go to Texas, but I had no intention of staying long term. I thought I would go there, learn everything I needed to know to win this battle, pick up the pieces of my life, and then start over. I thought it was as simple as that.

When my daughter and I arrived in Texas, it was a bit awkward at first for sure. But that all changed when my former father-in-law embraced me tightly, and with tears in his eyes, thanked me for having the courage to come. He drove us out to his beautiful ranch-style home. When I walked through the front door, I sensed an overwhelming feeling of love and acceptance from both him and his wife. The living room was set up as a church, every chair in order with musical equipment set up in front. He proceeded to show me to the bedroom where my daughter and I would be staying. I was so excited because it was connected to the church/living room. I felt like I was literally sleeping in the church.

As I became part of that church family, I learned so much so quickly. My emotions were like a roller coaster. People were patient with me as

I struggled through withdrawals of not having the drugs. I only had a few dollars to my name when I arrived there. I thought, *I have to save what I have to buy my last pack of cigarettes.* As the offering plate was passed one Sunday morning, something came over me, and I reached into my purse and put every penny I had in the plate. As it made its way to the row behind me, I thought, *Wait! What did I just do! That was all the money I had for cigarettes! I need that back.*

God is so gracious. He completely delivered me from cigarettes that morning. I have never even had the desire for a cigarette since that day. Praise the Lord! Only God could deliver like that. I had smoked for so many years. The desire was gone from that morning till this day around twenty years later.

I am so thankful that in the early years of my walk with God, the Lord made sure I was placed in a Pentecostal church. I am not sure I would have been able to move into the victory I needed without the awesome power of the Holy Spirit at work in my life. Shortly after accepting Christ and attending this church, I was baptized into the Holy Spirit. This empowerment made a huge difference in my walk with Christ. What would have happened if I had been placed in a spiritually dry place that lacked the power to drive the demonic out of my life? God knew what I needed.

AN IMPORTANT LESSON LEARNED

After having been in Texas for six months, I thought I'd learned all I needed to know. I was ready to go back to Washington and start a new life. I was so on fire for God. I felt like such a new person. I was convinced that when I went back there, everyone would accept the Lord. I just knew my drug dealers, my boyfriend, my sisters, my mom, and my dad would all accept the Lord Jesus into their lives. Then we would all live happily ever after! The dear couple I was staying with strongly encouraged me to be very wise in my decision about going back to Washington. They stated that even though I had so much zeal for Jesus, I should not expect that everyone would feel the same. They went on to explain that I was still a babe in Christ, and I might not be mature or strong enough spiritually and emotionally to stand alone.

I had no church to attend in Washington. I would not have

Christian friends, nor a family to support me there. But what about my son? What about all my possessions, my car, clothes, and what little furniture I had? Was I willing to lose everything once again? With so many thoughts running through my mind, I was faced with a life-altering decision. YES was my answer. The price I had to pay for this new incredible freedom was worth it. Jesus gave up His life for me. I would do nothing less for him!

ABOUT A YEAR LATER

After about a year of staying at my father-in-law's church, God moved me to another Full Gospel church in East Texas.

God was doing a mighty work in me. I realized, for the first time, that my whole life had been based on lies and deception. I was so ready to experience healthy emotions and a new way of life. The first and most difficult hurdle to overcome was the issue of forgiveness. I began to realize that the more unforgiveness I felt toward those who had hurt me, the more it was really only hurting me by producing anger, bitterness, and resentment in my heart. Somehow, I knew this was the first step in the healing process, and it had to start with me. Learning to forgive myself wasn't easy. Someone once told me to look at myself in a mirror every day and tell myself how beautiful my heavenly Father thinks I am. I was told to speak over myself how He has a wonderful plan for my life, and that He forgives me. I was told never to remember my past. For the first few months, I couldn't even look at my reflection in the mirror. I was so ashamed of myself. I struggled to understand how He could love me. Then I would fall on the floor and weep uncontrollably.

After a time, I was able to accept His love for me through the encouraging Word of God, a broken spirit, and hours each day on my face before the Lord. The Holy Spirit was empowering me and healing me. It's hard to explain, but all the anger, resentment, and unforgiveness I felt toward the people in my life had now turned to feelings of sorrow, forgiveness, and mercy. I realized that Jesus loved me so much. I began to understand that He forgave my sins, that I have eternal life, and I am to show that same compassion and forgiveness toward those who had used and abused me. There was a time that my own mother padlocked the refrigerator in the garage to keep me from getting food, after she found out I was sneaking in taking some. My own sister wouldn't give me firewood to keep my daughter and me warm during the freezing-cold winter. God had to help me, and I was able to completely forgive and love them.

I found myself often weeping for the lost souls in my family. I didn't understand intercession at this time in my life, but God had given me an intercessor's heart for my family. My heart was so heavy for my dad especially! I recall asking the Lord how I could be free from this burden that weighed so heavy on my heart. His reply was, *Write a letter.* I was surprised He really answered me. It wasn't an audible voice, but a strong thought that just entered my mind. So I sat down and wrote him a letter explaining how I forgave him for what he had done. I went on to explain how Jesus loved him so much and wanted him to accept Him so he could have eternal life in Christ. I sealed the letter and sent it off. The minute I put it in the mail an overwhelming peace came over me. I felt released from that burden.

I went on to make a videotape of myself explaining to my mom, sisters, and grandfather about how satan had been the ruler of our lives growing up. That's why we all had such messed-up families, but I found someone who could change everything we ever thought was right. Jesus is His name. I was sure this would change their way of seeing things. I wanted them to know the truth. I wanted the truth to set them free as it did me. After cutting off all communication with my family for over a year, I was excited to hear their response to the tape I sent. I heard back all right! They cussed me out and screamed at me. They said things like, "How dare you? We know how to live our own lives." I was so upset, and I couldn't understand how they could remain so blinded to the truth. I was so thankful to God for taking me far away from that place and time. My family now consisted of the people around me who showed me love, support, and guidance in the things of God.

I am *forever* grateful for the opportunity to have been discipled by this wonderful man of God. He and his dear wife opened their home to us, providing a safe place of refuge in a very critical time in our lives.

NO TURNING BACK

Now let's rewind a year. I decided to stay in Texas. I got a job and worked hard to make a new life for myself and my daughter. I held on to the hope that one day, when I had my own place, I would be able to take care of my family. I would have a stable home to offer my son in the event he would ever want to come and live with me. Unfortunately, his father was turning my son's heart against me. I had to work through forgiving everyone, but in Christ all things are possible!

I called my mom to tell her about my new life in Jesus, and that I had made the decision to stay in Texas. Her response was anger. She could not understand how I could serve a God I could not see. She was convinced that I was serving the wrong God. She went on to say how I always copped out of life, and like always, I would never amount to anything. One thing I had to learn and apply to my life was breaking curses off my life. The word curses my mother spoke had to be broken off my life.

My boyfriend's response was about the same. And I called my son to let him know I wouldn't be moving back but would work very hard to make enough money to see him as often as I could. His words cut deep into my heart as he said how much he hated me and never wanted to see me again. It cost me a lot to follow Christ. I literally lost all I owned and all my family and friends. I completely fell apart. All the same feelings I had when I lost my son the first time came rolling back in like a flood. It took me days, if not weeks, to recover from the reality of losing my whole family.

I worked hard to find a job and had some help buying a car. My former father-in-law had a pastor friend located in the same town in which I worked. When I would get off work, I would go to his church and pray. Falling on my knees and crying out to God there at the altar by myself brought me great comfort. I soon offered to clean the church for the pastor. Since I was there every day anyway, he happily agreed. I believe God gave me a servant's heart during this time in my life. Even if it meant scrubbing toilets and vacuuming floors, I felt it was such an honor. I thought, *God, I don't have much to offer you, but I love being in your house, and making it beautiful for you.* I remember a man I worked with was continually trying to date me. He was constantly making sexual advances toward me. By God's grace alone, I was able to resist the temptation. The old Sandy would have jumped at the chance to have an affair with a married man. But God was radically changing me. The purposes and "evil anointing" of satan were being canceled and destroyed off my life forever.

I recall leaving work every day before he would so I could go to the church and lock myself away in God's presence. He caught on to what I was doing and followed me one day at a distance. I didn't realize he followed me until I heard banging on the door of the church. Then he banged on the windows. He was trying to get in any way he could. I was terrified as I crawled under the pew and prayed, "God, please help me! I don't want this kind of life anymore! Please make him go away!" I never heard another thing from him after that desperate prayer. I went to work the next day only to learn that the man who had been pursuing me had quit his job. I was so relieved. I didn't have to face that battle any longer. Praise God for his protection! There is no temptation that has come to us that God has not provided a way of escape. His grace is truly sufficient for us.

STILL THE FIRST YEAR OF MY SALVATION

After about a year of living with the dear couple who took me into their home and loved me and my daughter as their own, I was introduced to the first Christian single young man I've ever met. Before that, I wouldn't allow myself to date at all. I was afraid to let my heart be drawn away from my first love of Christ. I wanted to be married and be happy with someone who put God first in his life. I desired someone who would protect us and who would teach us how to live this life of Christianity. When I met him, I thought, *This is the person!* He also had a son, who was a year older than my daughter. I felt as though I was given another chance to raise a son after losing my own. I was so very happy after we got married. I wanted my life to be based on having a godly family. I desperately wanted my daughter to be raised by a God-fearing man who would take care of us. I wanted someone to lead us in the ways of the Lord.

We moved to another town and attended a large church where my husband became the head children's pastor. This was that second Full Gospel church I mentioned earlier in this book in which I loved being in the presence of God so much that I offered to clean the church. I would spend hours on my face before the Lord. I believe the Lord saw my sincerity and brokenness. I had no idea, but I was not completely delivered yet. There were also subtle open doors in the life of my husband that would be devastating down the road.

With a sad heart, I write that this marriage did not survive. Because of my husband's sexual infidelity, we ended in divorce thirteen years later. This broke my heart because I know now as a Christian that God hates divorce. I will write more about this later in the book. Satan comes to steal, kill, and destroy, but Christ has come to give abundant life. Even though this broken marriage was a terrible chapter in my life, God has since brought great restoration and victory. It was during this marriage, before it ended, that God did a great work in my life.

During this thirteen-year period, I totally loved my new church, my new pastor, and his family. He became a spiritual father to me for around ten years. He was the one that baptized me and discipled me in the faith. He understood a lot of what I was going through. He also took my past very seriously. He helped me get stable. He and his family played a huge role in my life. Even though I had accepted Jesus as my Lord and Savior, I still found myself continually struggling on the inside to maintain this life of freedom. I would still experience demonic activity going on around me and violent nightmares. I counseled with my pastor for a couple of years.

One day, he simply told me that due to the severity of the demonic abuse while growing up, he regrettably was unable to help me any further. He very sincerely felt this was simply out of his league and his level of knowledge. He was a gentle, humble man who did everything he could to help me. I truly saw Jesus in him. He just didn't know what else to do to rid me of all the demonic forces at work in my life that refused to let me be completely victorious. He referred me to a professional Christian counselor.

I felt so crushed and rejected by my pastor that I made up my mind that I would not open up to anyone ever again. This was certainly not his intention. I should have taken this better, but I still needed inner healing as well. I thought, *I will just handle this on my own!* Unfortunately, this decision resulted in me not dealing with inner healing issues that would not be completely dealt with until much later in life. This left open doors to the enemy.

Looking back, I respect my pastor for being honest with me. I know that he loved me enough as part of his flock to admit he couldn't help me but tried sending me to someone who could. Really, what else could he have done? He and his family have played a tremendous positive role in my life. Words can never express my gratitude. I am still able to see him sometimes. Little did I know that much later on in life, he would play a very significant role in setting the course toward my destiny and freedom.

TRAITOR TO SATAN

During my childhood, I was literally dedicated to satan on an actual altar. There was a ritual performed dedicating me as a bride of satan. Because of my desertion from satan's kingdom to Christ, I was considered a traitor that must be destroyed.

While living in Washington State, I had been very sick at times with no medical explanation. I had gone to many different doctors, who ran a series of tests. Shortly after my third marriage, I received a call informing me that the doctor's office had been trying for months to contact me about some test results they received. They went on to say that I had precancerous cells located so deep within my female organs that they were almost undetectable. They highly recommended that I consult a physician immediately for treatment. After the results of a cone biopsy, I was told by the doctor that there had been so much sexual abuse done to my body at an early age that they recommended a hysterectomy. I was twenty-nine years old. I was really hoping for another child someday but was thankful that they detected the abnormality in its early stages. This was one area of spiritual warfare over my life, but it didn't take me down. There were many more areas of spiritual warfare I will discuss later.

A BURDEN FOR THE DEAF

As our happy family was forming, I was asked to teach a Sunday school class at my church. I was so excited and accepted this calling as a teacher for children. One morning a young girl around the age of six walked into my classroom. She was a first-time visitor and was deaf. *Oh God, I prayed, how do I teach her about you?* I had such a heavy heart for her. I literally had to step out of the room into another so I could seek and cry out to God for this situation. I got myself together and went back into the room to teach. At first I was yelling, thinking the child could hear me. The other kids told me, "I don't think it will help by yelling loudly!"

By the end of class, an amazing thing happened that would change my life and career. This little girl was sitting on my lap while we were singing "Jesus Loves the Little Children." She was feeling the vibrations of my throat and showing me the signs for the song. I fell in love with signing at that moment. I felt God was calling me to a deaf ministry. Do you know that I never saw that little girl again? I believe that was a divine appointment that morning for me. Here I am, twenty years later, an interpreter for the deaf. I had no professional training of any kind. The Lord helped me and blessed me in that, even just teaching myself, I picked it up very fast, and I have been able to work at universities with higher education.

My dear pastor had a local television program where he would minister a devotional once a week. He asked me if I would like to interpret for him during these times. I was very nervous at first. But as time went on, I became very comfortable on a platform in front of a camera. The Lord was using this to help me get comfortable being in front of people and ministering.

MY NEED FOR INNER HEALING, DELIVERANCE, AND DISCIPLESHIP

With my husband and I working full-time jobs, the ministry, the kids in school, and the kids playing sports, things became extremely busy and started getting chaotic. I finally had the opportunity to reestablish a decent relationship with my biological son. He was old enough at this time to fly by himself and stay with us for a few weeks during the summer.

Sadly, my husband and I gradually began to drift apart. I found some of my old habits starting to resurface. I had a lot of problems with control, strife, and sexually ritualistic nightmares throughout our relationship. I didn't know anything about Jezebel and Ahab spirits at this time, but this was a central issue in this marriage for sure. I had no clue how a healthy marriage or relationship with my children should be. I was never taught or shown what a normal family was. I had a tendency to manipulate most situations to get what I wanted, and I would withhold sex from my husband if I didn't get my way.

Things were once again becoming all too familiar. As sad as this is, to me this was a typical family! This was the ways of my family and the way I was raised. Strife was rampant in my family growing up. Disorder and division in the home was all I knew. Treating each other with dishonor and disrespect was common in my upbringing. I have learned so much since these days, and my life is completely different now.

A TURNING POINT

By this time in my walk with the Lord, I began to read various books on inner healing, deliverance, and generational curses. I started to learn about what I still needed in my life and how much the Bible speaks about the power of blessings and curses. Derek Prince has two books that profoundly affected my Christian walk: one is called *They Shall Expel Demons* and the other *Blessings or Curses: You Can Choose.* I also was given books by Rebecca Brown to read. I really related to these books.

How do I fight against what I cannot see? I recognized a pattern that had been passed on from generation to generation in my family. I remembered what that hooded figure at the foot of my bed was demanding. He was demanding for things to pass on to the next generation. This is a big deal with satan. Through Derek Prince's books I mentioned, I began to see that I was wrestling with unseen forces and barriers trying to keep me from my destiny in Christ. The enemy was bent on keeping me in a defeated posture. I learned there were nine curses (nine categories) listed for those disobedient to God's Word that travel down family lines. Nine is the biblical number for judgment. Also, there were seven major categories of blessings listed for those obedient to God's Word. Seven is the biblical number for complete perfection.

Leviticus 26 and Deuteronomy 28 are very clear about the blessings and curses of obeying God's Word or disobeying it. Once these passages are examined, one can begin to put into a list nine curses and seven blessings based on your personal response to God's Word. I could see in my family destructive relationships, especially with men. I could see Jezebel and Ahab tendencies and other signs of curses like

1. Humiliation
2. Barrenness, unfruitfulness
3. Mental and physical health problems
4. Family breakdown (divorce, family alienation)
5. Poverty
6. Defeat
7. Oppression
8. Failure
9. Disfavor

Satan was working overtime to try to keep these curses at work in my life since my family bloodline was dedicated to satan. I was specifically and individually dedicated to satan as well. But, I also began to understand Galatians 3:13, which clearly states, "Christ redeemed us from the curse of the law," and now I could be free from these things and move into great blessings in Christ! The seven blessings of obedience are

1. Exaltation and promotion
2. Health and long life
3. Reproductiveness and fruitfulness
4. Prosperity and success
5. Abundance
6. Victory over all our enemies
7. God's favor

I was beginning to see the need to break free from these curses and press into the blessings of God through faith in what Jesus did on the cross. I also could see in my life and my family serious problems with inner healing. There were issues with rejection by pushing people away, building invisible walls around ourselves, and serious insecurities. My whole family has been plagued with divorce, alcoholism, substance abuse, rage, hatred toward male figures, manipulation, health problems, and sexual sins. It truly saddens me, that to this day, satan has been allowed free reign to dictate the course of lives of the people in my family. As far back as I know, I am the first person in my family to dedicate my life to the Lord. My current husband is the first male authority figure that I know of in my entire family line who has truly lived for the Lord.

I was willing to break these chains (through the power and blood of Jesus) that have held my family captive for all these years. They *will not* continue to affect my life or my descendants from this point on, in Jesus' name! I declare victory over the enemy! I very literally had to be like a branch cut completely off from my family line and replanted as a new tree in Christ. The weapons to fight this war against the enemy of our soul had been freely given to me when I made up my mind to serve Jesus with all my heart. The warfare that we face is further discussed in 2 Corinthians 10:4 and Ephesians 6. It was only after a great trial that I went through that I was able to fully understand and put into practice what I was learning through the books on deliverance and the Scriptures in the Bible.

I was able now to start talking to people in my church about my past and the importance of not being ignorant of satan's devices (2 Corinthians 2:11). It was very difficult for the first year or so to tell about everything I had experienced. As I would start talking specifically about the demonic forces at work, I would always experience confusing thoughts, my body would begin to shake uncontrollably, and I couldn't get my words out clearly. It was unnatural. The enemy tried his best to keep my testimony from going forth. After all, we are overcomers by the blood of the Lamb and the word of our testimony according to Revelation 12:11. Some people thought I was over-spiritualizing things, and others were astonished at what I had endured growing up. It didn't matter to me what they thought. I had a responsibility to tell people about the dangers of witchcraft. I had to help them understand that things like Ouija boards, Harry Potter, and séances were not a joke. I had to warn them about the movies and music that promote the occult, extreme violence, sexual perversions, and chemical dependency (legal or illegal). This was not fun and games. These things at times might seem innocent, but actually they allow the enemy access to cause devastation in people's lives.

INIQUITY DRIVES

In Scripture, there are different words used for what we commonly just refer to as sin. *Sin* has become the generic term for disobeying God. In Scripture, however, we see the word *sin* is literally translated "missing the mark." The visual is an archer shooting an arrow and simply missing the target. It is implied that sin is not intentional or premeditated. *Trespass* is another word we see. This implies a line crossed that shouldn't have been. We put up "No Trespassing" signs to keep people out. This implies a warning not heeded and regretted. Then we see the word *transgression*. Transgression is literally translated "rebellion." Rebellion is when someone absolutely knows something is wrong, but with premeditation, and full knowledge, does it anyway. This is very serious. Eve was deceived and sinned, while Adam knew what he was doing and transgressed. Lastly, we see the word *iniquity*.

Iniquity is literally translated "bent, crooked, or perverse." This word implies something bent toward evil within a person. Iniquity drives are very real and very serious. Some people develop these drives through repetitious sin, but a lot of iniquity drives are inherited and aggressively travel down family lines. It could be a strong tendency toward sexual vice, an unhealthy fascination with the occult, substance abuse, or violent tendencies. Someone may not understand why they have this strange drive and tendency within themselves, but it is an iniquity drive. Pride is very subtle and is a huge issue regarding iniquity in people. Jesus not only paid for our sins at the cross, but very specifically we see he was pierced for our transgressions (outward bleeding) and bruised for our iniquity (a bruise is a bleeding inwardly). Jesus paid for these iniquity drives to be cleansed in us and the crooked places within us to be made straight.

For example, some members of my family struggle with addiction to alcohol. Even though I never enjoyed drinking, I would use it as an escape from reality at times. This was an iniquity drive in my life. I know full well that it would be disastrous if I were to give in to this desire. Not to mention the fact that it could cause other struggling Christians to think this behavior is innocent. Thus I could be a stumbling block to their salvation. We cannot be a stumbling block for others! That is a very serious warning in Scripture. We are accountable for our actions and who they affect. The way we dress, the way we talk, and what we do can affect many others who are watching our lives.

In Matthew 18:6–7 Jesus says, "If anyone causes one of these little ones—those who believe in me—to stumble, it would be better for them to have a large millstone hung around their neck and to be drowned in the depths of the sea. Woe to the world because of the things that cause people to stumble! Such things must come, but woe to the person through whom they come!"

THE BATTLE INCREASES

As word circulated about my testimony, I was contacted by a man in our church who was part of the Gideons International ministry. Since I was saved through a Gideon Bible, he wanted me to come to a local pastor appreciation meeting and tell my story and the effect God's Word had on my life. The meeting would consist of several pastors and Gideons in the area. The purpose of these sessions is to get pastors involved with the Gideons, who literally send Bibles all over the world and see countless salvations because of their ministry. These meetings are also a thank-you to the pastors who are already helping the Gideons by having them come to speak at their church or sowing financially into their ministry.

I can do this, I thought. *Just a few people sitting around casually talking.* I would attempt to accomplish that without shaking and stumbling over my words. When I arrived at the restaurant, I went inside and was directed to a back meeting room designated for the banquet. There, I saw what looked like a million people (really only 50 or so). My first instinct was to just turn slowly and walk back out, and then *run* to the car and leave.

The gentleman who invited me came up and pulled me in the doorway and introduced me to several people. He showed me where I was to sit (at the very front with other speakers for that evening). I was praying under my breath the whole time. I couldn't even eat the wonderful meal prepared for me. I was so nervous I thought I would be sick. They had a podium set up at the very front where I was to stand and speak to the group. I immediately pictured myself up onstage in front of the TV camera at church signing for my pastor as he delivered his weekly devotional.

Again, I thought, *I can do this*. God had been preparing me to be in front of people. It was just a brief thought, however. Then reality set back in, and I wanted to be sick. When it came my time to tell my story, my voice quivered and my knees were literally shaking. Good thing I had a skirt on so no one could notice! After about a minute, however, I was speaking with ease as I relived the past in my mind. Of course, this was the first time to open up about all the trauma of my past. I became emotional and started to cry. The Holy Spirit gave me peace, and at times, I felt He was giving me the words to say. It took me about 30 minutes to try to sum up my whole life because I knew we were on a schedule. By the time I was finished, I looked out toward the group, and people where weeping and clapping. Then they stood up and clapped. I was crying. They were crying. What had just happened? It was an amazing experience. I believe the Holy Spirit was right there with me the whole time. I couldn't have done that on my own. I knew that for sure.

As I prepared to leave, an older gentleman approached me and introduced himself as the Texas state overseer. He was the head guy of the state. He expressed how moved he was by hearing my testimony. He went on to ask me if I would be interested in having my name and contact information printed in an international Gideon list of testimony speakers. In short, this meant that any Gideon group internationally could invite me to come and speak at their banquets, conferences, etc. The only requirement was that I had to shorten my testimony to ten minutes.

Of course, I was so excited, and I accepted the offer. But how in the world I could sum up my whole life in ten minutes? I had no idea, but I began to work on it. It was like a flood gate opened up from that night on. Each time I spoke, I became more comfortable in front of a crowd and more and more dependent on the Holy Spirit. Unfortunately, I had to omit so many details of my life to keep it at ten minutes. Sometimes they would allow me more time. Other times it was less than ten minutes. I began to travel all over the United States. My husband at that time would come with me frequently. I felt so incredibly blessed to have been given this opportunity to share what my beautiful Savior had done in my life. It gave me an open door to minister one-on-one at times to people who had similar experiences.

IT ALL TOOK A TOLL

Over time, as God was using me with my testimony, my marriage was becoming more stressed. My husband began to be distant in our lives. He quit coming to my daughter's birthday parties and activities. We had been married for almost thirteen years. Divorce never entered my mind. I knew what God's Word had to say about the subject, and to me, divorce *was never an option*. The kids were entering their teenage years and were also showing signs of stress and fatigue. I really didn't realize the spiritual warfare that ensued as soon as I began to speak out like this.

I recall having a strange dream which occurred two consecutive nights. In this dream, I got up in the middle of the night and walked toward a huge mirror sitting on my dresser. I had a beautiful flowing white nightgown on as I looked at myself in the mirror and saw my reflection. I looked very sad. I just stood there for a long time looking at myself. Then I woke up. The second night, I had the same dream except for one minor change. As I looked in the mirror, I saw myself in the reflection wearing the same gown, but it had been torn, and my face was muddy, and my hair was messed up. As I looked closer at my reflection, that person began to break down crying. The crying was deep and uncontrollable. I was unable to stand and fell to the ground in great sorrow. Then I woke up very disturbed by the dream.

The pastor who was a spiritual father to me for around ten years had also left the church to pastor in another city. He is a wonderful man of God we still keep in touch with. The new pastor coming in was also a wonderful man of God that preached the Word and loved our family.

A GREAT TRIAL

While I was sound asleep one night, my daughter came into my room crying and frantic. She sat next to me, leaned down toward my ear, and said, "Daddy has been sneaking into my bedroom and touching me in my private areas." Half asleep, I sat up thinking I had heard her wrong. We went out to the living room, because my husband was sleeping next to me, to clarify what she had just told me.

I couldn't believe what I had just heard. *What!* I was caught completely off guard. As I held her, she cried so hard. I couldn't believe I had let this happen. I had no idea! I should have seen the signs! I never thought this could happen in a Christian family. I immediately woke my husband up and confronted him with these accusations against him. At first, he denied it, but when my daughter interjected, he said, "I'm so sorry." Unbelievable! This was really happening!

The next day, my husband and I went to our new pastor, who had recently replaced our previous pastor with whom I had counseled. My husband admitted that a similar incident had occurred several times previously with a young girl who was in our care for a short time. Although she never informed me, it was verified that it did take place. My husband willingly stepped down as children's pastor and was not permitted to come back into my home. I didn't know what to do next. I was completely crushed and somewhat irrational.

Word about this incident had circulated around my children's school and community. This resulted in Child Protective Services getting involved. After counseling with our new pastor, he suggested that I try to work things out to bring the family back together. I truly did want that, but I was having a very hard time trusting my husband. The thought of divorce had *never* entered my mind. I know God hates divorce, and so do I. I told him I wasn't sure I could feel comfortable with him in my home, especially at night while I slept. His answer to me was, "You could sleep with your daughter with the door locked to ensure this would not happen again."

I couldn't believe these words were actually coming out of my husband's mouth. CPS contacted me the next day and told me that if I allowed my husband back into the home, they would have no choice but to remove my daughter from me and put her in foster care. My husband's son, my beautiful little boy whom I had raised from the age of two, went to live with his grandmother. Once again, the enemy had managed to bring total devastation and great division in my life, and the son I loved dearly was ripped away from me.

NO OTHER CHOICE

Filing for divorce, going through the criminal charges brought against my husband, and trying to maintain stability for my daughter's sake was a very difficult task. As ordered by CPS, my daughter and son had to go through counseling, and I was trying my best to pick up the pieces of my shattered family and move on. I was unable to continue speaking for the Gideons during this time due to emotional, mental, and physical stress. It was all part of satan's plan to shut me down and render me ineffective for the sake of lost souls coming to know Jesus through my testimony. The Lord had blessed me with such a wonderful family and another chance to raise a son. That was the highlight of my testimony. Now, what was I going to say? This was a well-orchestrated attack by the enemy to shut me up.

I realized that the dream I just had just a few nights before was preparing me somehow for the brokenness I now felt. I also realized that the deep inner healing and deliverance issues in me had never been confronted and dealt with completely. Obviously, my husband had some open doors to lust and perversion as well. See, even sincere people can still need inner healing and deliverance. As painful as it was, I had to discover a way to be delivered completely from these demonic spirits that were working against me.

Every door to the enemy needed to be shut and every avenue sealed off so that I could live victoriously in Christ Jesus. He paid for me to be completely free, and up to this point in my Christian walk, things had been a struggle. I was unaware of the open doors in my husband's life that also played a significant role in the amount of control the enemy had in our family. Satan saw the weaknesses in the family unit and was able to steal, kill, and destroy! How sad. It is because of ignorance and vulnerability that most marriages and families are torn apart in this day and age in which we are living. The enemy is satan, not each other, and we *are* in a spiritual war. The books I was given to read were like seeds being sown to prepare me for complete freedom. It was as if all was coming to a head.

BEAUTY IN THE MIDST OF ASHES

After about six months, I was contacted by a woman who had heard my testimony. She gave her life to Christ because of my testimony, was water baptized, and was attending a local church. She had been deeply entrenched in satanism while growing up. Her story blew my mind. Her childhood was so much worse than mine. As a result, she was truly struggling as a Christian. Her family was deeply involved in satanism. She had been told her whole life that she was a "purebred" satanist, and therefore, Jesus would never accept her.

My testimony caused her to realize that that was a lie. Her family was threatening her life. They were deadly serious and could have accomplished this goal if it had not been for the grace and protection of Jesus. The coven that she once belonged to made it very difficult for her due to the strong relational ties she had with people, threats against her and her children, and personal death threats. She was married and had kids and desperately wanted to be free from the demonic. She wanted this not only for herself, but for her children as well. She wanted deliverance from the demonic spirits that continued to have access into her life. She was tormented.

I wasn't sure how to go about helping her. I reviewed the books I had read about this subject combined with my personal experience. I just knew that God wanted to use me to help her overcome all of this. She opened up to me because I had been through similar situations. Most of all, I knew what she was telling me was real. After much prayer and fasting, I agreed to meet with her for deliverance along with her husband and one of her friends. My heart went out to her as I sought God on my face praying for her freedom. As we all sat in the kitchen of her friend's home, I started to talk to the woman being delivered about specific names of spirits that had been operating in her life. I began confronting and commanding them to leave in the name of Jesus.

All was well at first. Then, as we continued, the woman's face became distorted while a man's voice came from her vocal chords. She literally stood up, grabbed hold of my neck with the strength of five men, and threw me up against the wall. Then she slammed me down onto the kitchen table while screaming, "Satan is king; he wins, and God loses." This frightened me. Her husband and friend tried to restrain her while calling out her name. I was binding the enemy in Jesus' name and, after a short time, she lost all strength and fell to the ground. Needless to say, that was the end of that session! I continued to work with her on a regular basis while taking the necessary precautions.

HER BREAKTHROUGH

I asked her to come to my church and attend one of our services. Afterward, we would all stand in agreement for her complete freedom while the pastor prayed for her. During the altar call, she and I went up to the front to receive prayer. This was a Full Gospel church, so I knew the pastor would deal with these issues. As the pastor, a few elders, and I surrounded my friend, we began to pray. As the pastor reached out to lay hands on her, a loud screech came from the young woman, and she started to swing her fists at the pastor. "Don't touch me!" she screamed.

All of us standing around her tried to restrain her as she fell to the floor, still reaching toward the pastor. Since I was her friend, I was told to try to speak to her while others were holding her down as she was writhing about on the floor. I leaned over her trying to calm her down. She grabbed my neck and in a demonic voice called me a traitor. "That's right," I replied. "In Jesus' name, you are commanded to leave!" She had the strength of several men. She was lifting grown men in the air with one arm. After prayer, her body went limp. She had regained awareness of her surroundings but had no recollection of what had just taken place. The pastor cast around twelve or more demons out of her that day! It was a powerful display of Christ's victory over the devil.

WHERE IS THE HEART OF COMPASSION?

I stood up and looked around at the congregation. Only those of us who were praying for the young woman remained in the sanctuary. People were scared and went out in the foyer area. They started making comments such as, "We will not tolerate this in our church." Really! Where in the world are people to go to be delivered and healed if not in the church?

Over time, this young woman and I developed a meaningful friendship, and she was on her way to freedom. Praise the Lord! Through my experience I can truly attest to the fact that born-again Christians who have been baptized can still have demons operating in their lives where open doors have not been dealt with and sealed off through the blood of Jesus.

Luke 22:3 states that satan entered Judas before he betrayed Jesus into the hands of the Pharisees. Judas was a follower of Christ and within his inner circle, but he was a thief which opened him up to the devil. My dear friend is a perfect example—not to mention the detailed description of my life as I have shared with you. Churches need to have ministries in place to help people like this. We need to be a New Testament book of Acts church! It is highly unscriptural to be afraid of the enemy.

MOVING ON

After the divorce was filed, my daughter and I began the long, hard road through the healing process. This was a difficult year for my daughter and me. I went to counsel with my former pastor, whom I respected very much. He was the same man who was a spiritual father to me, pastored me for ten years, and tried his best to help me in every way he could. He played a significant role in helping me to put everything in perspective. While there I was reintroduced to a young man named Scott who had ministered some at my church previously. He was also the person who had suggested that I read books about the deliverance ministry that included actual accounts of others' experiences such as mine. I also had traveled and given my testimony a few places in which he had ministered.

As I left the church, Scott walked me out while telling me about a ministry he was overseeing located in Rockwall. I had been looking for another place of worship mainly because some individuals at my home church were very good friends with my estranged husband. Even though he had openly admitted his guilt, they found a way to blame me and my daughter for what happened. Christians can be better than the world at kicking people while they are down. Some even claimed I made the whole molestation story up. Unbelievable! How do you think that made my daughter feel?

With all the gossip circulating the community, I felt it necessary to move out of the area and start a new life once again. Due to the circumstances, the son I had raised decided that I was not his mother. Therefore, he distanced himself from the only sister he had ever known, and from me. It not only broke my heart, but my daughter was forced to deal with not only losing her daddy, but also her brother.

FEELING LIKE GIVING UP

I was so exhausted at this so-called life. It seemed everything I got close to was stolen from me. The only one I could truly trust was my Jesus. He would never leave me nor forsake me. I knew there remained strongholds in my life that allowed all of this to continue, but I didn't know how to confront and deal with it yet. The books I was reading were the beginning of understanding these things.

I started to attend Scott's ministry. Honestly, it was so refreshing to be in a new place of worship and meeting new people. The power of God was very strong in every meeting. Pastor Scott was teaching along the lines of spiritual warfare in a way I had not heard before. Oddly enough, God had been preparing him to take on situations such as mine. I learned more and more about the freedom Christ paid for me to have on the cross. Faith and hope were rising within me. Every part of me began to yearn to have that complete freedom.

For the first time, I felt the call of God on my life to be a part of a ministry that would help to set the captives free from a life of witchcraft, the occult, prostitution, and substance abuse. I had no idea at the time, but my pastor knew Scott very well. He had told Scott he felt maybe we would make a good couple, and God might be drawing us together. Scott said, "I will have to hear from God about it." Up until this point, my focus in ministry was the deaf community. Now I started feeling a strong burden to see the captives set free.

LOOKING FOR DIRECTION

I started to travel with the Gideon's and again and felt strength and power that only the Holy Spirit could provide to get the word out about the dangers of the occult. I had so much to say!

Meanwhile, my daughter was struggling with unforgiveness as well as starting a new school. She began associating with the wrong crowd, and I was at a loss as to how to help her. Through my new church, my daughter attended a week-long summer camp. This was the youth conference connected to the Brownsville Revival of Pensacola. When she came back, I was amazed at the transformation that had taken place in her life. She told me that she had gone up for prayer one night, longing for healing from all the hurt and pain she was feeling. While someone prayed for her, she fell to the floor and had a true encounter with the Lord. She went on to say that she was out under the glory of God for around four hours. After getting up off the floor, she was completely healed, having truly had an encounter with the living God. Thank you, Jesus!

MINISTERING TO AN EX-SATANIST

I had introduced Scott to my dear friend I had been ministering to. She had come a long way in the battle with the demonic forces that manipulated her life from childhood, but I was at a loss as to how to proceed to the next level of freedom. Consulting Scott, we would counsel with her on a regular basis. I learned so much from just watching him and was amazed at the spiritual authority he would demonstrate while confronting the demonic strongholds that were manifested through deliverance. The healing that took place in her life was so beautiful to witness. She told me that for the first time in her life, she was able to feel. Her emotions were so unstable for the first few weeks after her deliverance and healing that she would just cry for no apparent reason. As her husband would attest to, it was obvious the Lord was doing a mighty work in her. A deep cleansing was taking place that caused beauty to radiate from her in the days that followed.

THE FINAL BREAKTHROUGH

I was finally coming to the place in my life where I could admit I was still in need of deliverance and inner healing. For the first time since counseling with my former pastor, I was able to confide in Pastor Scott, and as a result, he began to work with me dealing with inner wounds that had been suppressed deep within me for so long. We began to develop a close relationship, recognizing we had a common bond with one another. I had feelings for him, and he knew it. As he stated earlier, he wasn't going to pursue anything until he heard "straight from the Lord" to do so. I felt rejected at first, but he was just wanting to make sure he was following the Lord. He was definitely not like other men I knew, who would play games and weren't completely sold out to Christ.

His way of thinking was so unfamiliar to me. I couldn't comprehend such strict godly standards he had set for himself. He was very careful about what he watched on TV, in movies, etc. If we were going to be together, he wanted to make very sure that it was in a public place. He wanted to make sure to avoid the appearance of evil. He told me while in prayer for various needs in the church, he suddenly heard the Lord speak to him, saying, "Sandy needs a godly husband." He responded with, "Okay, I will pray for you to send her one." He heard the same statement a second time, and his response was the same. He heard the voice a third time and realized God was calling him to be my husband and father to my daughter.

He was shocked that God would choose him. He was hesitant because of all the hurt my daughter and I had experienced, and he also knew there would be gossip and slander. Scott was concerned about the pain of my past relationships with men and what was in my family. He would have to be willing to take on this spiritual battle that originated deep within my family bloodline.

Doing only what a God-fearing man would do, he sought out godly counsel. He consulted my former pastor, who knew me very well. His response was that he could really see God using Scott and I together in a powerful ministry. Remember, he was the one that first put the thought in Scott's head that we might make a good couple. He went on to say that Scott would be faced with definite challenges due to my background, but he thought Scott would be able to successfully lead my daughter and I in the ways of the Lord. The pastor felt Scott would face spiritual warfare directly connected to his relationship with me. Scott went on to seek godly counsel from his father, who agreed that if Scott believed he heard from God, he better listen. Then, he went to his spiritual authority about the matter. They also confirmed this was a move of God. Everyone was in agreement.

Before Scott and I were married, I was awakened one night by my dogs barking outside. To my horror, I looked outside to see several people in black robes coming onto my property. These were the coven members of the woman I was trying to help. They were trying to make good on their threats to kill me. All I knew to do was to pray. Something happened when I began to pray. My dogs became vicious, even though they were normally very gentle. They viciously attacked these people. I watched as these people frantically ran from my property and never returned again. Thank God for His protection.

A NEW CHAPTER IN MY LIFE

A few months later, after my marriage to Scott, we faced new challenges in our marriage. My daughter was facing her own difficulties, trying to grow in her relationship with the Lord while going to public high school. School is such a harsh environment for our children these days in which we live. I recommend Christian parents consider either homeschooling or a Christian education. We saw that she was bending under the peer pressure she faced on a daily basis. So my husband and I decided to homeschool her. It was the best decision even though my daughter didn't think so at the time. She can attest to the fact that pulling her out of public school saved her life. She has thanked us now, but at the time she was quite upset.

Scott worked diligently with me, confronting the demonic strongholds still at work in my life that were now manifesting themselves through anger and rage. At times, he would confront these spirits by name, and as a result, I would lose consciousness, and the spirits would hurl threats of death and destruction. They simply would not allow anyone to get close to me. They admitted being at work in my family for generations, and they had a right to since my ancestors had accepted them into their lives.

My husband refused to accept their lies and would command them, one by one, to leave my life in the name of Jesus. The breakthrough was tremendous, but there was significant warfare against my husband. Within the year, my husband had gained a lot of weight and became very sick physically. He was viciously attacked both mentally and emotionally. He couldn't sleep at night, and when he did, would wake up in a total panic attack.

I was very concerned but didn't know how to help him. After a time of fighting this battle together, we both became stronger, and the warfare became less intense as each open door to the demonic spirits was closed. My life was sealed off by the blood of Jesus!

My husband recovered, and our ministry was doing very well. Actually, the spiritual battle my husband faced was a lot more intense than just fighting my battles. There is a strongman over our region that was attacking him viciously, and satan's servants were using dark arts against him. Also, some in the church world were speaking negative words (curses) against us and our ministry. So this was literally a battle for survival. But God saw us through it!

My husband felt he almost died during this battle a few times. What we learned during these difficult dark days of warfare have served to be very valuable lessons I will share in the next chapter.

IN RETROSPECT

Looking back at the course of my life, I know now how generational cycles are able to continue down bloodlines. Most people don't know the spiritual war each person is faced with every day of their lives. Satan's plan is to keep people spiritually dead. Most Christians are pretty clueless to the literal battle we are facing, and many don't want to face that reality. They have the mentality that things have just been inherited and just run in their family. Accepting this is telling satan that it is okay to be at work in their lives. I refuse to accept this. I am a branch cut off from my family tree, and now Christ has planted me as a new tree. I have laid hold of what Jesus has done for me on the cross.

Ephesians 6 talks about this war that we fight against the principalities and powers. Paul gives us instructions on how to use the weapons in the spirit to overcome evil forces at work in our lives and families. I made up my mind that these curses that were on my life and children at one time, were broken, and no longer at work. From the time I surrendered completely to Christ, I stood firm in faith that these curses would not continue. Now there are powerful generational blessings at work in my life and family. This generational chain of curses has been broken, and my descendants will enjoy the life that Jesus paid for them to have at Calvary. No more addictions, destruction of men, destruction of relationships, demonic sickness and disease, or pain and sorrow! Jesus paid for total freedom on the cross.

Most importantly, we must teach our children to do the same. They must continue to walk in spiritual blessings and not curses! I would have never thought that God could turn my life of witchcraft and serving satan into a woman after God's own heart, ministering with my husband and pastoring a church together. What an amazing testimony of the power of the cross. Only God could do that! The freedom and victory in my life now are amazing!

By the grace of God, my husband is a strong man of God who by no means will compromise his convictions. I have seen that in him. In the ministry, there are many critics and liars that all pastors have to deal with. But, I live with my family and know their lives. They love the Lord and live a true Christian life. The determination to see this victory all the way to the end is what gives me strength to continue. I plan on seeing Christ set many people free.

MY MOM AND SISTERS

I have been reconnected to my sisters and mother. All I know to do is to live this Christlike life before them. I know they cannot deny the change in my life. I realize that I may be the only true Christian example they may ever see. I continue to see my biological son from time to time and my three beautiful grandsons. However, I truly pray that we will someday have a close relationship. I spoke to my dad a couple of times on the phone while he was sick and in the hospital.

When I mentioned Jesus, he hung up on me. The last time we spoke was while he was in the hospital on his death bed, and I called him. Hearing the respirator on the other end, I knew it was difficult for him to talk. So I took full advantage in asking him if he knew where he would go when he died. I heard heavy breathing, then suddenly he said, "I don't want to hear about your Jesus." These were his last words to me as he died that night. My only thought was that I knew when he hung up that phone, he would continue to hear my words in his mind. Hopefully, he made peace with God before entering eternity.

THE BLESSINGS OF FOLLOWING CHRIST

I am so very blessed now. I truly don't deserve all that the Lord has done in my life and continues to do. Being able to see my daughter love and live for Jesus is amazing. She will never have to know the pain of family alienation, having to live on the streets, prostituting her body for food and shelter, or being used and abused by people. Thank God that chain has been broken! I am sure she will face her own challenges in life, but one thing is for sure, she will always have a loving family to support and help her through it all. She is an amazing worship leader at church. Worship and prayer are passions God put in her at an early age. She is truly using the gifts God has given her for His glory!

I continue to travel the nations, preaching the gospel. God has truly opened the windows of opportunity. I believe we are living in the last days. *The 700 Club* through CBN has picked up my testimony, and it was featured on Halloween 2014. Through this avenue, the opportunity to share my story has increased dramatically. Many gave their lives to Jesus when the testimony aired on *The 700 Club*. I have also been involved in a local jail ministry in my area. It definitely provides me with a captive audience.

A FACE FROM THE PAST

My first experience speaking in a jail was one I will never forget. It set the beginning stages of the call God put on my life for the lost and hurting behind prison walls. I was invited by a precious lady affiliated with the Gideons to share my story with a few inmates in the small town I once lived in while living my sinful life. I agreed to go. As I entered the cell where I was to speak, about six ladies were waiting for me.

While looking around the room, I thought I recognized some-one. Then I thought maybe she simply looked like someone I had known before. I couldn't put my finger on it. She was looking at me in the same way. I dismissed the thought and proceeded to talk. I felt an extreme compelling by the Holy Spirit to speak about gener-ational curses on individual lives and families. At the conclusion, I was walking around praying with each lady. When I approached this particular lady, I asked her, "Do I know you from somewhere? You look so familiar." I asked her what her name was. When she told me, I just about fell over! "Joyce, is that really you?" I asked.

She recognized my first name from years ago, but obviously not my last name now. Fifteen years earlier, I would often go to her house and buy my drugs from her. She was my drug dealer from years past. I couldn't believe it! I recalled practically living there with her three small children. She stated how I looked so different now—like a completely different person!

I am a completely different person in Christ!

She started to cry uncontrollably while telling me that all three of her children grew up dealing drugs, were involved in gangs, and are all in prison. I held her tightly and cried with her. How devastating! The message the Holy Spirit inspired me to speak about that eve-ning was exactly what Joyce needed to hear. As a result of this prayer time, and witnessing the change she saw in my life, Joyce fell to her knees and accepted Jesus as her Savior that night. How beautiful a sight it was! Jesus never ceases to amaze me!

Another time in prison, I felt led to give my testimony, and a lady asked me to pray with her. She had been tormented by the demonic and knew it. As I prayed for her, she began to squirm and manifest demons as they were leaving her. The other inmates were scared, but they were also amazed as the power of God defeated satan that night.

I will give another testimony of a young lady who was saved through our ministry after living on the streets. She was delivered of demons, set free from eight diagnosed mental illnesses, and physically healed of Hepatitis C and a cancerous tumor as my husband and I prayed for her. She since went on the mission field. Her testimony has also been on CBN. God is amazing! If he can do these things through me, believe me, he can do it through anyone!

LIFE'S LESSONS

I have learned so much throughout this journey in life. I feel as though I have lived four different lives. After surrendering to the Lord, I was at such a loss as to the raising of my daughter and teaching her to have healthy relationships with people. I was especially at a loss about trying to teach her about those relationships that require lifelong loyalty and commitment. It was foreign to me to submit to my husband as to the Lord and to understand the natural order that God created for a healthy family unit to function properly.

In reality, America's standard for a God-centered family unit has been completely warped. How much more difficult a task do we as parents face in today's society than 60 years ago? The world, as we know it, goes entirely against the standards given in God's holy Word. In fact, our culture encourages rebellion against the order that holds the family together. It seems just about every show on television will make the husband out to be a fool, and you see the wife wearing the pants in the family. Most movies encourage rebellion against authority in some form.

The primary challenge I have faced is the love of God as my Father. It truly has to start there if I am to have any relationship with my husband. How can I trust that my heavenly Father will not hurt me like my earthly father did? At a very early age, when that trust factor was supposed to be established and played out through the course of my life, it was destroyed. I thought all relationships were based on what I had been taught.

I have witnessed this behavior played out throughout my whole family. I have seen marriages destroyed, families in turmoil, all male authority crushed under the heavy weight of women manipulating and controlling every situation. It was as though a powerful curse to destroy men was released against our family. The Jezebel spirit seemed to be running rampant in my family. It had to stop!

As difficult as it seemed, I was determined to break free from this generational curse. It had to start with trusting God for who *He* says He is in His Word. As far back as I have researched, I am the first truly born-again Christian to ever wholly surrender her life into the hands of the almighty Father. So I was the first to change the course of life for future generations. I declare that my descendants will know the truth, and they will live under God's blessings! The generational curses are broken!

I learned the hard way that this doesn't mean that we will not face our adversary, satan. In fact, he will persist even more as we are more effective for God's kingdom. So be it! I have no fear of him any longer. In fact, I'm angry at how he destroys families and lives. I may get knocked down at times, but I will stand up and fight with more force than before until my life ends on this earth. Through *Christ* who gives us strength (Philippians 4:13), we are called to overcome and conquer.

Completing the testimony section of my book has been a very emotional roller coaster. I was forced to stop and think about events that I had blocked from my memory, and some I tried with all that's within me to remember but could not. Many times, during the course of writing, I've had to just stop and break down in tears.

As I look back at where I was and where almighty God has brought me to in this life, it is amazing! The main reason for writing this book is that even though I have had numerous opportunities to share my testimony with others, I have never been allowed the time to tell my *whole* story.

We are in the end times. We are about to see the closing of this church age. I know that society as a whole will be faced with such darkness like this world has never known before. Satan knows his time is coming to an end, and he is blatantly making himself known to all people in every aspect of society. Every person will be forced to make a life-altering decision that will determine their fate in eternity.

When I am no longer here on this earth, I trust that the information contained in this book will help bring you to the saving knowledge of Jesus Christ and help you make the choice to give Him your whole life. After all, we are not in control of this unseen spiritual battle anyway. Please give your life to Jesus.

2

What I Have Learned

First off, I don't focus on satan. I focus on the Lord, and what He is doing. Satan was defeated at the cross, but we have to enforce that victory now through faith. Spiritual warfare is very real. The Bible warns us to not be ignorant of the devil's schemes. I want to share some keys to victory that people may not have learned in a typical church setting. My husband's book entitled *A Warfare Manual* is a complimentary book to this writing and has been added to this book. Also, our website (www.fnirevival.com) has an extensive listing of free teaching resources.

THREE STEPS IN DELIVERANCE

We have written a deliverance questionnaire and also one for those leading a deliverance session. This has been compiled through much research. Many Christians have varying degrees of satanic influence in their lives. This can certainly come from past sinful activity in life. Even though the sin has been forgiven, the results and bondage of that sin has never been dealt with completely. Unforgiveness is a huge door for satanic torment, fears, demonic health problems, and significant bondage to satan. Generational sin, curses, and spirits are very serious. They can travel down family bloodlines and torment for generations, if they are not dealt with.

Also, people can simply be oppressed by something they are around. So the questionnaire helps distinguish any open doors to the enemy. The primary goal of the demonic is to keep someone from ever accepting Christ as their Savior. After a person accepts Christ, the next big goal of the demonic is to keep them from ever being able to do anything for the Lord. The demonic wants to keep them defeated, struggling with sin, bitter, hurt, so sick they can't be productive, or impoverished and working multiple jobs to makes ends meet.

1. Cancel the enemy's legal rights.

There are three basic steps to effective deliverance. First, *cancel legal ground to the enemy*. What opened the door in the first place? What legal rights does the enemy have? Confession and repentance of sins, the sins of ancestors, and forgiving others will usually deal with most legal ground. Keep in mind that there might need to be renunciations of past agreements, pacts, oaths, or ceremonies either the individual or their family bloodline participated in. Sex is a huge door for demonic entrance and defilement. I have also heard that things like ungodly movies, music, to posters on walls have allowed demon torment to enter for some. We see many times in Scripture that we need to confess and repent of our sins. Satan loses his grip when we do this because the blood of Jesus washes us clean. It is incredibly important that we receive forgiveness and cleansing from sin by faith. Don't go by feelings. We may not feel clean or forgiven, but the Bible says God is faithful and just to forgive us of our sins and cleanse us from all unrighteousness if we will confess our sins. This is laid hold of by faith. Faith is a very important component to receive any healing or deliverance of any kind.

2. Destroy the works of satan.

The next step in deliverance is *destroying the works of satan*. As Christians we have authority over all the power of the enemy, as we see in Luke 10:19. We must lift up our voice and break every curse and destroy every work of satan. The words of our mouth spoken in Jesus' name have awesome authority over the enemy. Also, the power of the Holy Spirit is what destroys the bondages. I have learned that God's holy angels are of great help in deliverance. The main point here is to directly and specifically break any and all works of satan. There needs to be a confrontation with faith and boldness.

An example of this could be if someone has a curse and spirit in their life because their mother went to a witch for help. So after the person confesses this sin and renounces the witchcraft (canceling legal rights), then the oppressed person or deliverance minister can say something like: "I destroy any curse or work of satan that has been at work in this person's life because her mother visited a witch. I destroy this right now in the name of Jesus!" It's important to speak with faith and authority and not rely on feelings. These things are conquered through faith.

3. Drive out the demonic.

The third step to deliverance is *direct confrontation with demons.* You must always start with the strongman, or the others won't leave (Mark 3:27). Either the deliverance minister or the person needing deliverance can speak directly to the demon and say: "I bind you in Jesus' name. You no longer have a right to this person's life. The blood of Jesus is against you and has canceled your right. I command you to come out and go from this person now and forever. You will no longer have anything to do with them or their family." They have to leave. Again, it is essential to do all this by faith and not rely on feelings.

So we see deliverance takes place through (1) canceling legal rights, (2) destroying the works of satan, and (3) driving out the demonic.

The final point I would add is this: In John 10:10, Jesus states that satan comes to steal, kill, and destroy—He plainly reveals him as a thief. And Proverbs 6:31 says that when a thief is caught, "he must pay [back] sevenfold, though it costs him all the wealth of his house." I want you to understand that the demons should have to repair the damage caused, restore sevenfold what was stolen, take all they sowed in that person's life out, and put every disorder they created back in order upon their departure. This is significant.

I know a minister friend who commanded cancer to leave. It was a demon, but he added, "You must take all the cancer out of the body as you go." The person went back to the doctor and was reported completely cancer-free. Demons would love to just leave a mess when they leave. You can command them to put things back the way they are supposed to be and leave.

My husband once commanded spirits to leave someone at a home for teens. The demon left the person, but there began to be reports of people experiences paranormal experiences around them. So he learned to command spirits to leave the person, then go straight into the abyss. Afterward, this type of incident stopped. Demons will try to go to someone else, or they will try to linger around. You can command them to completely depart into the abyss and not go to anyone else.

REPLACING THE SATANIC

Only God can heal people. People can be wounded in their spirit, soul, or physical body. Only God can truly heal. The first step toward healing is forgiveness. My husband and I have had reports of endless counseling that never really brought change. We need the power of the Holy Spirit to bring true healing.

After driving out the demonic and destroying the enemy's works, it is vital to replace these places with blessings and what Jesus paid for us to have. I will explain a lot more about a deep consecration unto God in the next section, but let me give a few points here. Many people we have prayed with have had many curses and works of satan destroyed. One of the most powerful things that can happen to someone is for a father to speak (not just pray) a blessing over them. This is all through Scripture. Even in the New Testament, Jesus blessed the little children that were brought to him (he didn't pray for them or prophesy over them).

Even to this day, Jewish families will have a father speak a blessing over his wife and children every Sabbath. We have examples of blessings on our website. Usually, my husband, or some other male authority figure, will stand in proxy as their biological father and speak a father's blessing over them. This is replacing the curses that were once there. Blessings are extremely powerful. A curse will hold people back, but blessings release them into God's destiny and purposes for them.

I heard a powerful testimony of a man who had a bad heart but blessed his heart daily. He would lay his hand on his heart and speak something like this: "I bless you heart to be healthy and strong and function perfectly." After a year or so, he went back to his doctor. To his doctor's amazement, a creative miracle had changed his heart according to exactly what he had spoken over it.

I have heard of marriages and family relationships restored by speaking blessings. Blessings empower, release life, and bring about positive change, and angels enforce blessings. Begin to speak a blessing over your spouse, children, home, and overall life on a regular basis. Things will change! Sometimes because people haven't been taught better, they are very negative with what comes out of their mouths. Without realizing it, they are cursing so much of their lives. This is legal permission for demonic oppression.

I am so incredibly thankful that God put me into a Full Gospel church right after my salvation. They taught me the truth of the need to fully repent of my sins and have a holy fear of God. I shudder to think where I would be today if I were in a different church, one teaching me that I could live in sin and still go to heaven. I am also so thankful that right after my salvation, I was baptized in the Holy Spirit and received my prayer language.

Where at one time demons were at work in my life, now the Holy Spirit has filled those areas and given me strength. The change was remarkable. There were still some areas in which victory was not complete until I married Scott, because no one knew how to help me cancel that legal ground. But the strength and power of the Holy Spirit was what kept me going. Also, after Scott got me delivered, the anointing and infilling of the Holy Spirit increased in my life radically. The Holy Spirit seals us. He can fill us, envelop us, and protect us. He leads us and teaches us the things of God. He also empowers us and uses us. Those who are getting delivered will be somewhat vulnerable if they don't have the empowerment of the Spirit of God.

A DEEP CONSECRATION UNTO GOD

There is a much deeper understanding to what we call sacraments in church. The church, for the most part, is ignorant of the true power of *communion, water baptism,* and *anointing with oil.* However, I have found that all three of these scriptural patterns for cleansing are extremely powerful and can result in a deep consecration unto God, healing (spirit, soul, and body), and deliverance from the demonic realm and its works.

1. Communion

Let's start with the communion table. The elements obviously represent Jesus' body and blood. My husband has done two series entitled the "Priesthood of the Believer" and "Communion Hebrew Roots" in which he deals with these issues in depth. He also has a sermon on the Lord's Last Supper, which is an illustrated sermon helping people understand the power of what was actually happening at the Last Supper the Lord had with his disciples when he instituted holy communion. These are all on our website for free.

The communion table is seen in the tabernacle of Moses as the table of showbread. The pattern was weekly eating of the bread then replacing it in the tabernacle. The early church "broke bread" weekly, which I believe was also the communion table.

I know of a woman who had a wayward son who was very rebellious. Their relationship went from serious strife to estrangement. The son had become deeply involved in the occult, drugs, etc. In prayer, the Lord spoke to her that there was "one lamb per household" at the Passover in Egypt. She knew the Lord was showing her that as she took communion, it would also affect her son. So she did so by faith. Something broke in the spirit realm. He called her, crying, shortly after that. He gave his life to the Lord, and their relationship was healed.

So what is the mysterious power of communion? Abram had promises but wasn't seeing them fulfilled. In Genesis 14, Abram won a war with four kings with only the men of his household. This was God's supernatural victory. Melchizedek came to Abram as a priest, and they took what we know today as communion together. Melchizedek then blessed Abram. Right after that encounter, God appeared to Abram and changed his name, gave him the promise of Isaac, and instituted the covenant of circumcision. Something was released into Abram's life when he took communion and was blessed by an authority figure.

The priests of the Old Testament had a picture and type through the animal sacrifices of what we know today as communion. We have the fullness in Christ of what they only saw through the eyes of faith. Even the Old Testament priests were consecrated by eating of the sacrificial offerings, and the Bible states anything the sacrifice touched became holy (Leviticus 6:26–27). If you would like a deeper study on communion, you can go to our website and listen to a series entitled Communion Hebrew Roots. Here are some basics of what happens when we take communion:

- Deep consecration unto God takes place (Leviticus 6:26–27).

- Applying the blood of Jesus to the doorpost of our lives and families brings great protection from the enemy (Exodus 12:7).

- Many are healed while taking communion and remembering that by His stripes were healed (1 Peter 2:24).

- Many are delivered as they remember Jesus paid for their complete deliverance on the cross, and His blood sets them free (Galatians 3:13–14).

- Increased revelation of the Lord comes like never before (Luke 24:30–32).

- Increased strength for the battle will come (1 Samuel 21:6).

- Entering into God's presence in an awesome way, because the blood is what takes us into His presence (Hebrews 9:12).

2. Water baptism

Next, I want to discuss the power of water baptism. Most Christians, unfortunately, struggle with a lack of knowledge. Hosea 4:6 warns us that God's people perish because of a lack of knowledge. This is simply because they aren't hearing a lot of things preached in typical churches across America. First Corinthians 10 describes Israel's Red Sea crossing as a "baptism into Moses." Now think about it for a moment. God was deeply consecrating them. First, they had Passover in Egypt. We have Holy Communion today, which is basically the same thing they were doing at Passover. We just have the fullness now on the other side of the cross. Then the Israelites were baptized in the cloud (baptism into the Holy Spirit) and the sea. This is also what we know today as "water immersion." This was all a preparation to see God appear to them at Sinai.

The same water that baptized God's people was the same water that closed behind them separating them from their sinful past (Egypt) and destroyed the enemy that was trying to chase them into their future. Many people who come to Christ still have a lot of baggage. Water immersion helps to destroy that and remove it from their lives. I have personally known of people getting healed and/or delivered of demons in water baptism. In fact, during the last baptism we held, we had at least two get delivered of demons, others got breakthroughs in their lives, and everyone told me they felt very different afterward.

Without getting too deep with this, it was during a ceremonial Passover meal (Pesach Seder) that Jesus instituted Holy Communion. It was as if he cut out a piece of that ceremonial meal and gave it to us to eat and drink all year around. He also washed the disciples with water during this ceremonial meal. He was preparing them for their encounter with God at Pentecost. Just as Moses gave Israel Passover, then the baptism through the Red Sea, so they were spiritually ready to encounter God's power at Sinai.

A deep consecration unto God helps set us completely free from the devil and prepares the way for us to have deep meaningful encounters with the Lord. Naaman, the leper, was healed during self-immersion (2 Kings 5). Jesus had the blind man wash the mud off his eyes with water, and he was healed (John 9). The angel would stir the waters of Bethesda (John 5), and the first one immersing in it was healed.

Immersion was a very common practice in the early church. They understood the power of water baptism. I cannot find one place in Scripture that states water immersion is meant to be a "one-time only" experience either. We need to quit adding or taking away from Scripture. I believe the rule of thumb should be, whenever it is needed, let's make it available for people. Our church has a twice-a-year corporate baptism for those who want to consecrate themselves fresh unto the Lord. Most people participate, and there are numerous testimonies of healing, deliverance, and powerful change. This is always after a corporate time of fasting we do as a church.

3. Anointing with oil

The next thing I would like to discuss is anointing with oil. The Old and New Testament are loaded with references to anointing with oil. We can clearly see in the Old Testament that priests were consecrated through blood, water immersion, and anointing with oil (Exodus 29). This same pattern has carried over into the New Testament today.

Mark 6:13 speaks of Jesus' disciples being sent out to minister: "They drove out many demons and anointed many sick people with oil and healed them." First John 5:8 shows the blood, water, and Spirit testify and are in agreement.

Anointing with oil helps to consecrate people, places, or things as holy unto God. My husband has taken communion in our home, put some juice on the doorpost, and poured some out on the ground of the property to consecrate it as holy. He has also anointed the doorpost of each room of our home as holy unto God. We see this pattern when Moses anointed the tabernacle in Exodus 40. This is why, in the New Testament, James teaches us that the elders of the church (authority figures) could anoint a person with oil, and the prayer of faith would release healing into them. If they have sinned, it would be forgiven them (James 5:14–15).

When reading the Old Testament, you need to understand Jesus came to fulfill it. What Israel was given in the natural, we are given in the spiritual now and have the fullness in Christ. For example, the priests were given specific holy garments in which to minister. We are now priests unto God (1 Peter 2:9) and wear spiritual garments of salvation, righteousness, power, and glory. You cannot see these spiritual garments with the natural eye, but they are there, and they are real. The Jews had to only eat kosher foods in the Old Testament. Now we are only allowed to feed on what spiritually is beneficial for us. If you are feeding on spiritual garbage all the time, you will suffer tremendously. Be wise about what you watch on TV and movies, what music you listen to, where you spend your time, and who you spend it with.

A STRONG PRAYER LIFE

I cannot express enough how important it is to maintain a strong prayer life. My husband did a series on "Going Deeper in Prayer" that teaches how to have a powerful prayer life. Excellent books have been written on the subject as well. Two highly recommended books on this subject would be *Prayer that Brings Revival* by Dr. Cho and *Could You Not Tarry One Hour* by Dr. Larry Lea. Prayer is the source of strength to individuals, families, and churches. A praying church is a powerful church. In fact, the first thing witches that infiltrate churches are taught is to remove any corporate prayer from that church. That shows how much of a threat it is to satan. Jesus said clearly his house is to be "a house of prayer" (Matthew 21:13). Jesus put the emphasis on prayer as we gather together for services.

I love God's Word and read it daily, but that is the extent of what most Christians do and call it prayer. Sadly, many Christians are too lazy to even read the Bible anymore. Reading the Bible is vitally important, but it is not prayer. Memorizing Scripture is also vital to our spiritual maturity, but it is not prayer. Prayer is communion with God, fellowship with the Holy Spirit, and resting in the Lord's presence. I don't know where I would be today if it weren't for having a strong prayer life. I have learned a lot of this from my husband. I pray this will stir all those reading this to press into a powerful, effective prayer life.

James 5:16 in the Amplified Bible says, "The earnest (heartfelt, continued) prayer of a righteous man makes tremendous power available [dynamic in its working]."

SHIFTING ATMOSPHERES

There are climate atmospheres in the natural. In the far south there is an atmosphere that is favorable toward palm trees. These would not survive in the far north of our country. In the same way, your home and family have a spiritual atmosphere. Unfortunately, there are many Christians plagued with negative, strife-filled, spiritually sterile atmospheres in their homes. Our homes should be a place of God's manifest presence. This will come when we make our homes a place of taking the Lord's Supper and speaking blessings. When we fill our homes with anointed worship and prayer, then the presence of the Lord will invade our homes. Our homes should be in spiritual order where husbands are leading into God's purposes, wives are submitting to their husbands, and children are obeying their parents. Then the blessings of heaven can flow freely.

A very negative atmosphere can fill a home that has any occult, Freemasonic, or idolatrous paraphernalia of any kind. If there is profanity, cursing, and fighting, the atmosphere becomes sterile. Children can wither in that environment. Where there is lust, and entertainment that breeds lust, the atmosphere is shifting into a sexually unclean place that will be absent of God's presence. In fact, demons can enter a home because of the occult, idolatrous objects, and sexual sins taking place there. The movies and television of most families are loaded with extreme violence, lustful scenes, occult activity, and profanity. This releases defilement into homes. Let me add that things that cause bondage—like alcohol, gambling, pornography, and tobacco—can create an oppressed atmosphere as well.

Just like palm trees in the North would wither and die, many Christians are withering and dying spiritually because of the atmosphere of their homes and families. If we will go through our homes and clean house, then begin to do the things that please the Lord and bring His presence, the atmosphere of our homes will radically change. I know the Lord desires the spiritual climate of our homes to promote spiritual health and well-being. If you feel the enemy has invaded, lift your voice in the name of Jesus, and command him to leave your home after you have cleansed it. We have a download on our website about cleansing and sealing off property and homes. I can attest to the effectiveness of this, because my home has peace and God's presence in it. It is a place where it is easy to pray and worship.

FEASTS OF THE LORD

The book of Galatians clearly shows God's strong condemnation for anyone trying to find righteousness or salvation through works or returning to the law. In other words, we are no longer saved by the blood of animals and keeping the strict commandments of the law; rather, we have our salvation through faith in what Christ did at Calvary. Christ fulfilled the law. He didn't throw it away. I think many people view the Old Testament as something to be discarded, but Christ fulfilled it (Matthew 5:17). When we understand that, we can get a depth of understanding regarding the new covenant we live in. I wanted to make that clear up front. Many have not heard the truths I am about to talk about. In fact, most of Christendom, as we know it, has deep roots in the Catholic church's heritage rather than our Hebrew roots. This is a foundational issue that needs to be corrected.

Reading through the Scriptures, one begins to see that Paul spoke of keeping the Passover feast (1 Corinthians 5:8) and how he was planning to travel back to keep Pentecost in Jerusalem (Acts 20:16). At the same time, he clearly stated we do not have to keep the feasts (Romans 14:5). It is something that we can choose to do if we desire to do so as Christians. So what could be the benefits of keeping the Sabbath and Feast days?

First, let me show you something that really impacted my life.

"You cannot drink the cup of the Lord and the cup of demons too; you cannot have a part in both the Lord's table and the table of demons" (1 Corinthians 10:21).

My family had sat at the table of demons. This brought a powerful generational curse upon the whole family. The Lord's Supper that we celebrate and call communion was taken directly out of the Passover ceremonial meal celebrated by Israel every year. The cup we drink is the third cup of the meal known as the cup of redemption. The bread we eat was the afikomen bread that was hidden (buried) and later found. There is a depth in understanding the feasts. They give us a much deeper understanding of Christ and the Bible. They are also a prophetic timeline of God's timetable for the church age.

My husband felt it was important for us to start keeping Passover as a family and the church we pastor. The people love it. Every year we do an illustrated sermon of the Lord's Last Supper. It was like the Bible was coming alive to us in a new way. The first time I sat with my husband and daughter as we celebrated Passover, I felt something very powerful happen to me. It was as though God was replacing the fact that my family had sat at the table of the demonic, and now I was sitting at the table of the Lord and reverencing the blood of the lamb. There was something significant that changed in me that day.

I believe the Sabbath and feasts bring blessings upon us. Just like sitting at the table of demons brings a curse, I believe these bring a blessing. I encourage you to read Exodus 12 then Exodus 23 in the New King James Version. Also, remember that Jesus kept Passover and all other feasts. Here are seven blessings that come upon us when we keep Passover:

1. God will assign an angel to prepare the way for you. *"Behold, I send an angel before you to keep you in the way and to bring you*

into the place which I have prepared" (v. 20) and *"For My Angel will go before you"* (v. 23)—divine guidance!

2. God will be an enemy to your enemies. *"But if you indeed obey His voice and do all that I speak, then I will be an enemy to your enemies and an adversary to your adversaries"* (v. 22)—divine protection!

3. God will give you all that you need. *"So you shall serve the Lord your God, and He will bless your bread and your water"* (v. 25)—divine provision!

4. God will take sickness away from you. *"And I will take sickness away from the midst of you"* (v. 25)—divine health!

5. God will bless your fruitfulness. *"No one shall suffer miscarriage or be barren in your land;"* (v. 26)—divine abundance!

6. God will give you a long life. *"I will fulfill the number of your days"* (v. 26)—divine life!

7. God will bring increase and inheritance. *"Little by little will I drive them out from before you, until you have increased and you inherit the land. And I will set your bounds from the Red Sea to the [Mediterranean] sea, Philistia, and from the desert to the [Euphrates] River. For I will deliver the inhabitants of the land into your hand"* (v. 30–31)—divine victory over the enemy!

For even Christ, our Passover, is sacrificed for us. (1 CORINTHIANS 5:7)

There are books devoted to teaching people about the feasts. Robert Heidler wrote a very powerful book entitled *Messianic Church Arising*. I highly recommend! My husband said that book was truly life changing for him. Unfortunately, our Reformers were anti-Semitic. This resulted in some serious foundational flaws in the Christian church today. There is a very good movie entitled *Let the Lion Roar* that I highly recommend you watch. It exposes the dangers of these Catholic roots in the Christian faith that believe in replacement theology. We cannot even understand end-time prophecy without understanding Israel properly. Perry Stone also has some excellent materials along these lines. We as a church and family celebrate these feast times together. We do it in a very nonreligious way, seeing it from a New Testament perspective of being fulfilled in Christ. It has been a great blessing to us. We don't celebrate Halloween, and we make sure Christmas and Resurrection Sunday are about the Lord, not other distractions.

A SABBATH'S REST

My husband also began to lead us to keep a Sabbath unto the Lord— not in a legalistic way or a religious bondage, but as something that he felt simply pleased the Lord and would bring a blessing on our family. For 3,500 years Israel has kept the Sabbath. Again, none of these are obligatory for salvation or righteousness, but I propose to you today they do have value. John had the Lord appear to him with great revelation on the Lord's Day, which is the Sabbath (Revelation 1:10). Here are three very powerful blessings in Scripture for keeping the Sabbath.

> "If you keep your feet from breaking the Sabbath and from doing as you please on my holy day, if you call the Sabbath a delight and the LORD's holy day honorable, and if you honor it by not going your own way and not doing as you please or speaking idle words, then **you will find your joy in the LORD**, and I will cause you to **ride in triumph on the heights of the land** and to **feast on the inheritance of your father Jacob**. For the mouth of the LORD has spoken." (Isaiah 58:13, emphasis mine)

In my situation, I felt it was beneficial for me to do things the Bible says would bring blessings on me, my family, and my descendants. I have noticed a huge change in my life and family.

What do the Jewish people do?

First, let me say this is our heritage as Christians. The Catholic church is not our heritage. Christianity sprung up out of the soil of the Hebrew faith. Our roots are Hebrew, not Catholic.

The Jewish people will light two candles (symbolically one to remember the Sabbath and the other to set it apart as holy) on Friday night (their day begins at evening) to initiate the Sabbath. From that point on, they observe the Sabbath for 24 hours. The light of the candles represents the light of God's glorious countenance shining upon us, and his presence entering our homes. Then the husband/father will cover his wife and children under a prayer shawl and speak a blessing over them. Songs can be sung and prayers prayed at this time.

The next 24 hours are set apart as a time of rest, enjoying prayer, and spending quality time as a family. On Saturday night there is a Havdalah ceremony held that closes out the Sabbath. One can take communion with your family at both the beginning and end of the Sabbath. Havdalah is a beautiful little ceremony rich in meaning.

My husband uses the Havdalah time to consecrate us as holy for the upcoming week by taking communion with us, anointing us with oil, praying over us, and blessing us. What an awesome way to start a week! We are consecrated and empowered for the coming week and whatever it holds.

I have noticed, since we started keeping the Sabbath as a family, that the blessing and favor of the Lord are on what we are doing. Second, I noticed a sense of refreshing spiritually, mentally, emotionally, and physically. Finally, our family really bonded. I believe family healing and bonding is another blessing associated with the Sabbath. There is a website entitled hebrew4christians that has a lot of helpful information about our Hebrew roots as Christians.

CLOSING

I pray these lessons have been a blessing to you and will help you go deeper in Christ. The main thing that will matter in eternity is our winning souls here and now! Let's be soul winners for Christ and start sharing our faith like never before. The coming of the Lord is near. The signs show we are living in the last days. The Lord said His house will be a house of prayer. Let's get back to prayer. Prayer is what will change communities, families, and bring lost loved ones to Christ. Seek the Lord's presence and his shining glorious countenance upon your life. Let us live a holy and pure life before him. I want his manifest presence filling my life. How about you?

I now invite you to be blessed by reading my husband's book that will delve deeper into the warfare we all face as Christians and give you the tools and insight to be an overcomer. His book is a wakeup call for Christians. It will expose satanic agendas and things going on, even in the church, that many are not aware of. Let's pull down every stronghold and press into the last day anointing.

PART 2

A Warfare Manual
By Scott Boyd

I dedicate this book to:

The Captain of the Hosts of the armies of God
JESUS THE CHRIST

Preface

When the Lord first spoke to me about writing this book, I was in prayer. I had received prophecies, and ministers talked to me about writing, but I didn't really pursue it. I waited for God's timing. I have been in ministry myself for several years. I have been in the role of teacher, pastor, and evangelist, so I know the ins and outs of these roles. I have experienced rejection, betrayal, discouragement, and the feeling of wanting to get out of the ministry. On the flip side, I have also experienced revival and the rewards of seeing lives changed in the ministry. This life of serving Jesus is an exciting, difficult, and bitter-sweet ride, but well worth it.

I hope this book will bring encouragement and challenge us all, because very few really reach their highest potential. Most fall very short. My goal is to teach in love, but to also encourage personal studies on certain subjects. That is why I will reference specific books in various chapters that I feel will have a tremendous impact on you, the reader. I do not intend to reinvent the wheel. There are such good writings already in the body of Christ on spiritual warfare and deliverance. I have read all the books that I reference and feel they have changed my life. I hope this will be more than just a book, but a manual that guides you into deep studies for yourself on these particular topics. Ultimately, no one can teach or bring revelation like the Holy Spirit.

I asked an elderly minister who God used mightily in my life if he had any advice for a young minister. He said, "Learn to pray." I would say getting to know the Holy Spirit as your best friend and having a strong personal prayer life are keys to seeing the higher purposes of God fulfilled through your life.

I have prayed for every one of you who are reading this book. It is not an accident that you are reading it. This is a divine appointment. Hopefully our paths will cross one day. May God bless you as you read.

In the love of Jesus,
Scott Boyd

Introduction

Deception

The one thing that will mark the end times will be deception. In Matthew 24:4 Jesus states, concerning the end times, "See to it that no one deceives you." In reading all the predictions in the New Testament of the days to come, the word *deception* is used a great deal. I believe this will be one of the greatest dangers of the end times. Deception is in every form of government, society, and even the church. We must guard ourselves against this great evil. I will try to lay a foundation in this book, hoping it will keep many from the deceptions that are here, as well as those which are coming.

One thing I will try not to do is make great predictions of what is going to happen in the near future. Many great Bible teachers have fallen into the error of trying to read into current events through the lens of Bible prophecy. God has given us a blueprint, but the details will unfold in His timing. We can get insight into some relevant current events, but we will always be looking through a prophetic glass dimly (1 Corinthians 13:12). One of the greatest guards against deception will be humility. One who is humble is able to admit he is wrong, and he is also very teachable. Traditional views of the end times have some holes in them. Many of our fathers in the faith have done a great job of laying a foundation but could only see in the light given them during their day. We walk in a greater light today, and those who come after us will walk in a greater light than we do now. The Bible says the path of the righteous grows brighter and brighter (Proverbs 4:18).

Also, Peter makes a prophetic statement when he says, "Until the day dawns and the morning star rises in your hearts" (2 Peter 1:19).

The closer we get to the Lord's coming, the greater the light of revelation will be. Therefore, we need to be open to new revelation as long as it lines up with sound doctrine. We must be walking in the present light we have been given without trying to see more than the Lord is showing us right now. This is a reason for many misinterpretations of prophetic Scripture in history—and today. I heard a great Bible teacher I love and respect say he is absolutely certain that the antichrist will be Muslim. The way he was speaking would indicate that he believed Islam would be the world religion of the revived Rome. It seems to me he might be reading into current events. Let me be clear that I am not saying he is wrong, but I am making a point that current events need to be evaluated but not read into Scripture. Many believed Hitler was the antichrist. He obviously was not, even though there are similarities. I have met people who take a certain road of thinking, and even though it proves to be very wrong, they will defend it to the death because of their pride. We must be humble to avoid being deceived today and in the days to come.

Also, I must state that we must keep the main thing, the main thing. So what is the main thing? The main thing is *Jesus*. He must be the center, foundation, and head of our lives and ministries. I have listened to some ministers, whom I love, go into such extremes in their teaching. I have especially seen this in the area of faith and prosperity teaching. I do believe in faith and prosperity, but there are gross extremes in this teaching today. How do ministers get into error to the degree that any passage of the Bible has to do with money? I believe that many started with sincere hearts and balance, but their eyes got off Jesus and onto a truth. This is the reason for much of the wrong teaching in the body of Christ today. *We must stay close to Jesus in prayer and keep our eyes on him.*

I believe focusing on a single truth, instead of the *Lord of truth,* will bring extremes in teaching quicker than anything. Even true prophetic experiences of dreams, visions, or words of knowledge can lead to deception if doctrine is made from them. Doctrine must be based on Scripture, not experiences. If an experience ever contradicts

Scripture, it must be thrown away. Using experiences to create doctrine are how many cults have begun.

Here is an example of what I mean by someone who took his eyes off Jesus and was led into deception. I had the honor of praying with a young man who was a practicing satanist. He truly came to Christ and renounced satan. I tried to explain to him that he may have been a "big shot" in the world of satanism, but he was coming into peon status in Christ's kingdom. I also explained that the way to move into greatness in Christ's kingdom is by washing other's feet (servanthood). Well, he started out well and was reading some incredible books by Rebecca Brown to help him. Her writings have changed many lives, and I highly recommend them. The only problem with the young man was he kept his focus on satan, and warfare, instead of Jesus. Consequently, he got lifted up with pride and rebelled against leadership. His focus should have been on his relationship with Jesus and being transformed into the image of Jesus.

If we will keep that focus, we will be okay in the days to come. When we get our central focus on something else other than Jesus, deception will soon follow. This is where most of the extremes in teaching have come. Someone got overzealous about a truth and took his eyes off the Lord and focused too much on that one truth instead of the Lord of truth. Remember, we are transformed by beholding the Lord's glory (2 Corinthians 3:18). Whatever we behold we will be conformed to. The last thing we want to do is put our focus on satan and what he is doing, thus being conformed to that. Let's keep our focus on Jesus.

Great power, signs, wonders, and supernatural things are on the horizon. This can result in some of the greatest deceptions the world has ever known. This is why I feel compelled to write this book. If we are not careful, we can make what the Lord is doing an idol. Revival, signs, and the miraculous can become an idol if we are not careful. Our worship must be to the Lord, not what He is doing. Many today in the West completely deny anything supernatural. How foolish! Even in Christian circles, this is true. But God is a supernatural God, and what He does will be supernatural.

We must be open to the new things He is doing, while testing the spirits to make sure they are of God (1 John 4:1). I believe incredible angelic visitations, dreams, visions, being caught up into heaven, seeing miracles, and power unprecedented even in the Word of God are coming. In John 14:12 Jesus said that we will do "even greater things" than He did! This day is upon us. We must be open to this, or we will miss God. But we must test the spirits to make sure it is not demonic. This will require discernment on an unprecedented scale.

Walking in true discernment is not being suspicious of everything. We must learn that.

Many have missed revivals and great things God had for them because of suspicion and criticism. True discernment comes from walking very close to the Lord. I get up every morning and start my day with a couple of hours in prayer. I also have learned the Word of God for myself, and I study it regularly. This is how we walk in discernment. If we are intimate with the Holy Spirit daily, knowing His voice and presence, we will certainly know when another spirit is present. Some Christians have gone to revival meetings that were of God and said, "A strange spirit was there." Well, the Holy Spirit was the one present, but they are so accustomed to the presence of religious demons, the Holy Spirit's presence was strange to them.

I will go into more detail on some of these issues in this book. Every time God has moved, there have been mighty critics that rose up and were used of satan to deter people from the move of God! These people caused many to go to hell and prevented many from receiving what God had for them. Be careful who you are following. Are the people you are following going after a move of God's Spirit? Are they hungry for God? Do you see Jesus in them? These are things that you need to ask, while not being critical of people who are imperfect. We are all a work in progress. If you sow grace to others, you will receive grace for yourself. This will take wisdom, discernment, and having the true heart of Jesus for people.

These are dangerous times to be a stumbling block to revival. God's heart is for the harvest, and it will take a mighty move of the Spirit to bring in the harvest. The last thing you want to be judged for is being a stumbling block to others. In the days we are entering, God will send his angels to remove stumbling blocks to his purposes (Matthew

13:39–42).

Looking at the fruit of people is so important in the days ahead. We must look for the true anointing on God's servants. Those who are appointed by man, or have raised themselves up through politics, will lack the true anointing. They will turn to manipulation, intimidation, and control in their leadership. This is witchcraft and must not be tolerated. There must be fruit in their ministry of people getting right with God, healed, delivered, baptized in the Holy Spirit, and taught the true Word of God with power.

Another thing we must look for is not just the anointing but character. The anointing is great, but if there is a lack of character, a fall will come! *Do the leaders live holy lives? Do you see the fruit of the Spirit in them?* This is vital! If not, I would say you probably need to move on to where this is true. I certainly don't want to ever write anything that would sow any discord in the body of Christ. God hates that (Proverbs 6:16). At the same time, leadership living holy and having the fruit of the Spirit is too important to overlook.

Those who are out of church will be likely to be connected into the body of the antichrist. If you are not in Christ's body, you will be in the body of the world. The greatest way to ensure not being marked by satan's mark is to have the mark of God spoken of in Revelation 7:1–3. It is vital to be knitted in a local fellowship somewhere and submitting to that authority. If you have been hurt, get over it and in church. I have been very hurt in church, but that is the way things are right now. We must shake it off and move on.

One thing I see is a transition in the Spirit. Look at the parable in Luke 10:38–42. In this story, Martha was so caught up in serving the Lord that she neglected his presence and fellowship. Mary, on the other hand, sat at his feet while he was present. There will continue to be a great division that will only get worse between the "Mary" church, which is going after Christ's presence, and the "Martha" church, which is about programs.

I felt the Lord reveal to me that in the past he sent "hot coals" to dead churches from various revivals. These are those who had the wisdom and humility to go where God is moving and receive of the anointing. They became flames of fire that were sent to dead churches. The Lord was sending them, hoping they would be a catalyst for revival in that church. I felt the Lord impress me these days are over. "Martha" has had time to repent. These hot coals are being removed and gathered into prepared wineskins in their area where they are understood and accepted.

I heard a prophecy that persecution toward Christians would begin in America in 2004. Praise God! Maybe this will wake up this sleeping giant! Persecution makes the church strong. I first thought that this persecution would come from the world and the media, etc. But after prayer, I believe the main persecution will come from the Martha church. These religious Pharisees will be jealous of the power, fruit, and success in the Mary church and will violently persecute them. So we must be ready for this. Many in the body of Christ have so focused on the book of the Lord, they do not even know the Lord of the book. This must change! Knowing the Scriptures is incredibly important, but we must draw close to Jesus and get to know Him. My desire is to be closer to Jesus and more like Him today than yesterday!

Friend, keep going after God. Don't ever stop running after Him. Stay on fire for God. Don't lose your first love! The lukewarm will fall away in the days to come. We must get on fire and stay on fire!

1

The Jezebel Spirit:
The Bride of Satan

In the day and time that we live in, the level of spiritual warfare is greatly intensifying. This is especially true for ministers. One of the greatest and most deadly attacks will come from a Jezebel spirit. There are already some incredible writings on this subject. I would like to recommend *Spiritual Warfare* by Richard Ing, *The Three Battlegrounds* by Francis Frangipane, and *Unmasking the Jezebel Spirit* by John Paul Jackson. In this book, I will be making references to other writings. One of my intentions is to go in depth on some subjects, while only touching on others. This book is meant to complement the other awesome writings that are presently available to believers. Later in this chapter, I will give you some keys I have learned about how to defeat this spirit. But first, let's talk about Jezebel and Babylon.

The Jezebel spirit is the most subtle, in-depth, and lethal of all spirits in my opinion. In Zechariah 5:5–11 we read of the woman in a basket called wickedness. She was pushed back into the basket until the proper time. I believe this is the Jezebel spirit. She has been held back and hidden until these last days. She will make her full manifestation in this last day move of satan in the earth. In Revelation 17 the Jezebel spirit is seen as the great whore of Babylon. Babylon means "confusion." Natural Babylon is what we know as modern-day Iraq. It is the place where the garden of Eden once existed. Also, Nimrod defied

God's command to fill the earth and multiply by trying to stay in one place united. He led a rebellion against God by building a tower to reach into heaven in an attempt to dethrone God and set himself up as God. So God caused them to all speak in different dialects to force them to fulfill his command to fill the earth and multiply. Thus, the tower was called Babel, and this is where Babylon gets its name. So we see that natural Babylon is a place of great rebellion. The Jezebel spirit can be summed up this simply: *It is the spirit of rebellion.* You have not been in ministry long if you have not seen rebellion in the church.

Natural Babylon depicts spiritual Babylon as well. In Revelation 18:2 we see the fall of Babylon. The Scriptures say, "Fallen! Fallen is Babylon the great!" The reason it says fallen two times is because natural Babylon will fall, and spiritual Babylon will fall as well. Spiritual Babylon is *the evil world's system that satan is the god over.* Jezebel sits as his bride or queen over this system.

SATAN'S END-TIME ARMY

Also, in Revelation 17:3 we see the whore riding a red beast with seven heads and ten horns. The seven heads represent the seven main world rulers of the end time. World rulers are the highest-ranking satanic spirits in the earth. Satan has given them authority to blanket the whole planet with their influence. Richard Ing records that among these are the spirits of Jezebel/ Ahab (rebellion), the Antichrist, Pride (Leviathan), Witchcraft, Mind Control, Murder/Violence, and Death/Hades.[1] I personally believe these to be the seven that satan has chosen for his end-time plans. The ten horns represent the ten main principalities he has chosen. Principalities are powerful fallen angels that have thrones over geographic locations. We see Jerusalem called "Sodom and Egypt" in Revelation 11:8 because these principalities are enthroned there. In Daniel 10:20 Daniel records his vision and the angel told him: "Soon I will return to fight against the Prince of Persia, and when I go, the Prince of Greece will come." These are the principalities over Persia and Greece.

THE HOUR IN WHICH WE LIVE

It's interesting that in the book of Revelation, Babylon and Israel are in the forefront. Iraq (Babylon) and Israel are on the news daily right now. We are certainly living in the last days. The Prince of Persia is over modern-day Iraq, Iran, Saudi Arabia, and Afghanistan. We are facing this spirit powerfully as revival comes to the Middle East, and America seeks to establish democracy there. This spirit will soon take a back seat as Europe unites, and the Prince of Greece will rise to its power. It will work with the Prince of Persia, forming the old Roman Empire. The prince of Greece will also work with the other eight princes in the earth, but I believe the Prince of Greece will be the most powerful of all. The same spirit that assisted Alexander the Great to conquer the world will assist the Antichrist in his rise over the European Union and the world.

QUEEN JEZEBEL: SATAN'S BRIDE

The main point is that Jezebel sits over all of this as queen. The red beast is the Ahab spirit that she also dominates. Just as the Father and Son have the precious Holy Spirit, satan has the Jezebel spirit. This is the spirit of the present world's system that is opposed to God. Jezebel seeks to turn men into women, women into men, and bring disorder into families. This is a blatant rebellion against God's ordained order and authority. Jezebel knows that if she is successful in this, she can destroy society at its most foundational stage. She seeks to bring rebellion into the church into these last days. The Jezebel spirit is not some little demon that possesses a few people here and there. It is one of the most powerful world rulers that blankets the whole earth with its influence. It will work with the prevailing principality over an area to defeat a church. Rick Joyner said the reason God moves certain men or women of God to a specific area is because their gifting and anointing is directly opposed to the prevailing spirit over that area. This is why they can be so effective, but many gradually become more and more conformed to the spirit over that area and lost their effectiveness. Men of God be ready. It will take very strong men to deal with this spirit.

STRONG MEN OF GOD: DECISIVE LEADERSHIP

My pastor tells an incredible story of a great man of God in our time. This great man of God has hosted one of the greatest revivals of our time. My pastor was speaking for him in the 1980s. We will call this great man of God Pastor Jim (not his real name). After the worship service, Pastor Jim said he had to take care of something before giving the microphone to my pastor, who was there as an evangelist. So Pastor Jim takes the pulpit and asks a family to rise. He said to the father of the family:

"Bob (not his real name), I have come to you in private to try to get you to repent of all the gossip and slander you have spread in this church. After you wouldn't repent, I took witnesses with me. We did everything to try to get you to repent. You have sown discord in this church. So because you refuse to repent, you are officially excommunicated from this fellowship. You are no longer members of this church, nor are you welcome to attend services. Now gather your things and leave."

After Pastor Jim said that, some ushers helped them out. My pastor (the evangelist) said it was like a black cloud lifted off that church. What this great man of God did was exactly what the Bible says to do in Matthew 18:15–18. There are times excommunicating someone is appropriate and Biblical (1 Corinthians 5).

Someone who has an issue with a Jezebel spirit will try to kill prophets, destroy their husbands (if they are women), and rebel against God-ordained authority figures. Sometimes the dogs simply have to lick their blood because there is no repentance. Strong, decisive ministers are the type of ministers who will be able to deal with this spirit. To defeat this spirit, you will have to be willing to go with God no matter what! We must go with God even if it means losing a congregation. If a minister is unwilling to do so, the congregation has become his god. Some will not deal with issues because they are afraid of losing money in the church! Money has become their god. How many ministers are really willing to go with God no matter what?

John Kilpatrick was the pastor of Brownsville Assembly of God in Pensacola, Florida. This church hosted the great Brownsville Revival. Steve Hill was preaching and said that during the first two weeks of the

Brownsville Revival, there arose some who did not want the revival. The revival was only two weeks old. It was a baby. A few of pastor John Kilpatrick's closest friends rose up against him. These were people he vacationed with. He loved them. But they led a rebellion against him, stating if he didn't call off the revival, they would leave, take others, and all their money with them. The next night in revival, Pastor stood, leaned on the pulpit, and stated, "This church is going after revival! If you don't like it, there's the door." Several left the church. However, millions of lives were transformed because he was willing to go with God—even if he went alone.

Are you willing?

JEZEBEL'S TACTICS

The Jezebel spirit uses manipulation and intimidation to control churches and ministers. We must be decisive men and women of God who are willing to take a secular job and lose members if necessary to be in God's will! Just like in Pensacola, the reward of going with God is always worth the price that will have to be paid.

Occult veiling

Jezebel's greatest strength is being hidden. That is why this spirit hates the prophets. They reveal her. Most of satan's attacks are hidden. I will discuss witchcraft later, but to make a point now, you will very seldom have a witch coven come to your door and say, "Hi, we are cursing you and your church." Usually, it is done in secret. The obvious reason is, if you do not know it is happening, you will not take authority over it.

We read in Revelation 17:5 that the whore of Babylon had "MYSTERY" written upon her forehead. She is a mystery because none see her (Isaiah 47:10).[2] This is her strength. Even if you approach someone in love, if that person has a serious issue with a Jezebel spirit, they will not receive you exposing it to them very well. They may cry at first, but that is only a manipulative maneuver to get you to feel sorry for them or think they are repentant.

This battle is truly won in the Spirit first before talking to people. If you preach on this subject, you will literally see some people squirming in their pews. If you say the name Jezebel, it will cause many to feel uncomfortable. I have had people say to me, "I wish you would use another name for that spirit." Why are they so uncomfortable? It is obviously an issue with them. We see God dealing with this spirit in Isaiah 47:2–3: "Take off your veil. Lift up your skirts, bare your legs, and wade through the streams. Your nakedness will be exposed, and your shame uncovered." Also in Nahum 3:5: "I will lift your skirts over your face. I will show the nations your nakedness and the kingdoms your shame."

This is how God deals with Jezebel. He exposes her. When she is truly exposed is when she begins to lose her power over people. Just as I have read from prophets in the Bible concerning this spirit, it will be the prophets of today that reveal her. The job of the prophets is to reveal, but the responsibility of the authority figure is to deal with this spirit once it is revealed. Just as Elisha anointed Jehu. Elijah had already revealed the deception, but it took Jehu as king to deal with Jezebel in 2 Kings 9–10. An authority figure would be like the husband of a home or the pastor of a church.

The Jezebel spirit uses witchcraft in the same way a witch or warlock would. Just like many ploys of satan are hidden, this spirit hides behind a literal veil. Remember, in Isaiah 47:2 God says, "Take off your veil." The word occult means "hidden or concealed." This is what attracts people to the occult who are looking into spiritual things. The mystery of the occult causes people to be curious about it. It is like a viper in the shadows that is not seen. Someone will reach for it in ignorance. It strikes, and then someone will have spiritual poison running through their veins and need deliverance. Likewise, Jezebel will use witchcraft magic to place a spiritual veil between herself and those she is working against. They don't see her even though you might.

I have shared with people who obviously had an issue with this spirit. *They absolutely did not see it at all.* They really felt I was wrong. Jezebel depends heavily upon this occult veiling. It protects her tremendously. Once a prophet rips the veil back and exposes this spirit, it will be up to the authority figure to do something about it. We read in Revelation 18:23: "By your magic spell all the nations were led astray." Also, Nahum 3:4 reads, "All because of the wanton lust of a harlot, alluring, the mistress of sorceries, who enslaved nations by her prostitution and peoples by her witchcraft."

She is known by occultists as: "Queen of heaven," Isis, Lilith, Astarte, Asherah, or Diana. She is the goddess worshipped by wiccans and pagans.

Direct attacks

Now I want to discuss some of her attacks.

Blatant rebellion. This spirit will cause people to lead a revolt against a man or woman of God in leadership as the leadership is going after God. I will go into more detail about what I am about to say in a later chapter. Let me say this now: if you are truly going after God with all your heart, you will attract satanic attack. You will offend people. If you are preaching the true gospel and the true Word of God, you will offend some people. You must be ready to deal with rebellion like Jesus said to in Matthew 18:15–18.

Bringing depression. The second way this spirit will attack is bringing depression upon someone. Jezebel uses a *spirit of discouragement* released upon a leader to bring like a black cloud over the individual. The goal is to cause the leader to feel like giving up.

Mind control. The *spirit of mind control* is the next spirit Jezebel will use. It tries to lock people into its way of thinking. There will come severe confusion and indecisiveness to someone being attacked by this spirit. Usually, there will also be headaches with this. This spirit is like an octopus with many tentacles. These tentacles go into several people's minds at one time. The goal of this spirit is to be like a puppet master. It will try to cause everyone to move with its satanic thinking. Witches have a spell they use to "cage" people. It is used to put blinders on someone and cause them to simply agree with everything the witch says. It literally puts their minds into a caged way of thinking. This is witchcraft mind control. It is very real and must be guarded against.

Manipulation, intimidation, and control. I mentioned the use of manipulation or intimidation (fear) to control people. A life that is crucified with Christ will not give in to such tactics. I would also say to look for this spirit to travel in family bloodlines. It seems to grow stronger with each generation. Also, people with this spirit will hang around others with this spirit.

As I stated at the beginning of this chapter, I want to complement other writings out there for the body of Christ. There is so much more I could say on this subject. I have only scratched the surface. I pray you will go into a deep study for yourself. This is a subject that needs to be thoroughly studied by all of us who are called into ministry. If you have not faced this spirit yet, you will, many times in the course of your ministry. We have a book entitled *The Jezebel Spirit* you can read on our website.

SEVEN SCRIPTURAL STEPS TO DEFEATING A JEZEBEL SPIRIT

I was spending some time with a minister friend of mine. He is a missionary to America. We were discussing different writings offered on these subjects. It is so remarkable to read three or four different views on the same subject from different authors. This is why I encourage other writings. I believe this brings a blossoming of truth. Here are some things I have learned dealing with this spirit. Believe me when I say, I have had a few encounters with Jezebel.

1. Confession and repentance

It is vital that we check our own hearts for any form of manipulating people, intimidating others, lusts, rebellion, or controlling others. Job 22:30 says, "He will deliver even one who is not innocent, who will be delivered through the cleanness of your hands." You will not be able to deliver someone else until you are free yourself. As ministers, we must live above reproach. I am amazed at the number of so-called Christians who can sit through ungodly television or movies—things that have nudity, sex, witchcraft, excessive gory violence, or foul language. Can you picture Jesus with a bag of popcorn, watching this filth? I don't think so! Some ministers wonder why there is no real anointing on their lives. Make sure to live holy, my friend. Guard what goes in your eyes and ears. It is so important to keep you heart very pure. For out of it flows the streams of life according to Proverbs 4:23. In Revelation 18:4, a voice from heaven says, "Come out of her, my people, so that you will not share in her sins, so that you will not receive any of her plagues."

2. Fasting

In 1 Kings 19:15–16 the Lord spoke to Elijah after confronting Jezebel and said, "Go anoint Hazael king over Aram. Also anoint Jehu son of Nimshi king over Israel, and anoint Elisha son of Shaphat from Abel Meholah to succeed you as prophet." I believe there are three very powerful revelations here. Prior to this, Elijah had gone on a forty-day fast. Of course, that length of time in fasting is probably not going to be necessary. I believe fasting plays a powerful role in all spiritual warfare. In Luke 11:21–22, Jesus teaches us, "When a strong man, fully armed, guards his own house, his possessions are safe. But when someone stronger attacks and overpowers him, he takes away the armor in which the man trusted and divides up the spoils." Fasting causes satanic spirits to be weakened by removing their armor in which they trust. After the armor is removed through fasting, the enemy is vulnerable for someone stronger to come in and destroy his works and replace them with the works of Jesus.

3. Allied force

Going back to 1 Kings 19, Hazael, king over Aram, was the first person Elijah was commanded to anoint. The country of Aram was an allied force to Israel. Their armies fought with Israel. I would like to point out here that it is so important to not try to take on Jezebel alone. Remember how Elijah was afraid and ran from Jezebel. In 1 Kings 18:3-5 we see he went *alone* into the wilderness. He became so depressed that he was suicidal. This was more than just having a bad day. The power of witchcraft was strongly coming against this man of God. He needed to be around the people of God to agree with him in prayer and encourage him. Jezebel will try to isolate you and then pick you off like a sniper. Build an allied prayer force when under attack. Stay around the people of God for encouragement. A major key to victory is to stay around the people of God for encouragement.

4. Standing in authority

In this scripture we go on to read that Elijah was to anoint Jehu as king over Israel. This man of God was the type of leader who would conquer a Jezebel spirit. He was very strong and authoritative. In 2 Kings 9–10 we read of how he destroyed the whole house of Ahab. He showed no mercy and left no stones unturned. He knew he was king and that God was with him. So he stood in his office and took care of business. We must be very strong in our dealing with this spirit. Please remember that we are fighting demons, not people. We are tenacious toward demons, but *firm* and *loving* toward people.

5. A fresh anointing

Last in this scripture, we read that Elisha was to be anointed to succeed Elijah. Elisha's ministry was marked by the great anointing on his life. When dealing with Jezebel, we need a fresh touch from heaven. This is the time to get hands laid on you for a touch from the Lord. This extra boost from heaven will help carry you through the battle that is ahead. In 2 Timothy 1:7 we read, "God did not give us a spirit of timidity [fear], but a spirit of power, of love and of self-discipline." The first thing to overcome an attack of intimidation from the enemy is power. In 1 Corinthians 4:20 Paul writes, "The kingdom of God is not a matter of talk but of power."

We need to continually walk in a fresh touch from heaven. This comes from having a strong prayer life and by being in places where God is moving in a powerful way. I will talk about impartation later, but I will say that there are some places that God is depositing his presence in these last days in a powerful way. I encourage you to go and receive prayer. There is an anointing in this. I know that my life and so many others have been totally transformed by receiving prayer at places like Airport Christian Fellowship in Toronto or Brownsville Assembly of God in Pensacola, Florida. There are other places as well. I know about the awesome power of God in the Benny Hinn meetings or Rodney Howard Brown meetings. Because I am not a Pharisee, you will always hear me encouraging people to go after God. Stay hungry, humble, and on fire.

6. Love

The next thing Paul mentioned that we need is love. We need to love God more than our reputations or what man thinks of us. We are to live crucified with Christ. A dead man does not care what people think of him. Ministers, above all, have to lose this care of what man thinks. This is the quickest way to be intimidated. If we truly love the

Lord, the fear of man will disappear. Paul also says that if he was living to please men, he could not be a bondservant of the Lord. In dealing firmly with people, it is important to not be in fear of what man's opinion is. This leads me to the next and last point.

7. A sound mind

Our minds are at peace when we know that we have the mind of Christ in a certain situation. The Bible says that "we have the mind of Christ" (1 Corinthians 2:16). We are all the body of Christ together. Therefore, no individual has the full mind of Christ alone. We need each other. It would be wise to seek counsel from wise leaders and get their opinion. This can ensure that your ideas are lining up with the will of Jesus perfectly. When you know that you have Christ's mind in a situation, there is tremendous boldness and confidence.

A PERSONAL EXAMPLE

There was a time when the Lord spoke to me to confront someone in a leadership position of a "ministry" that was in obvious hypocrisy. God had me ministering to some young people under their care for over two years. There was a move of God in the form of healings, deliverances, and revival. This gave me a platform to speak into the lives of leadership. The leader happened to be a woman (although a Jezebel spirit can be in a man as well). I first went into the office of this person to ask why people under her leadership were drinking, using drugs, living worldly, and sleeping around on weekends (to name some things). The leader said she had been doing this "ministry" for 16 years and that I didn't understand her ministry.

Then a time later, I noticed the way she wanted everyone to submit to her but could not bring herself to submit to her husband at all. So I asked her about this, giving detailed examples. She was obviously backed into a corner because of the specifics I gave. So she shed false tears to make everyone feel sorry for her and manipulate the conversation so that she was back in control. I had watched her gather her leaders in her office and try to intimidate all of them so she could control them. After I confronted her in love, she lied about me behind my back and persecuted me greatly for my stance. I had gone to her in private. I was so concerned that I was on a fast for that ministry.

I came in deep love and humility, and I left quietly. I figure the Lord will deal with them. I still love and care about them deeply. The Lord had told me that she was operating in a Jezebel spirit and to confront her about this. I felt by the Holy Spirit's prompting that it would not be received. But I knew I had heard from God about confronting her. I consulted with my spiritual fathers, who felt the same way I did. After I knew that I had the mind of Christ in the situation, I had boldness to speak up. Even though I was persecuted, God used me to shed some light into the darkness. If you know that you have the mind of Christ in a situation, it brings boldness to speak up.

These are some basic steps I have learned in dealing with a Jezebel spirit. I have seen people use threats and fear tactics to control others. I have seen others use seduction and manipulation to get their way. These are all classic profiles of someone under the influence of a Jezebel spirit. This spirit is sly and crafty. It knows how to make leaders look like the bad guy while making the person controlled by Jezebel look like the victim.

I want to close this section by talking about Matthew 18:15–20. Jesus teaches here on how to deal with problems in the church. I want you to notice verses 18–19: "I tell you the truth, whatever you bind on earth will be bound in heaven and whatever you loose on earth will be loosed in heaven. Again, I tell you that if two of you on earth agree about anything you ask for, it will be done for you." Notice that Jesus equates the problems in the church with spiritual warfare. That is why he mentioned binding, loosing, and prayer.

Satan is behind all division in the body of Christ. We should seek to see anyone who is repentant restored gently into the church. We should seek unity. I want to see walls of racism, denominations, generations, and between male and female come down. Jesus desires us to be in unity. I know in the city in which God has placed me there is so much competition and division between churches. Satan sits back and belly-laughs at the foolishness of Christians. If we can come together, satan knows he doesn't have a chance. That is why satan works so hard to keep us divided.

In John 17:20–21 Jesus prays that his people would be one as he and the father are one. We are far from that! Psalm 133 shows how unity brings the flow of the anointing. Let's seek unity in the body. There are times for confrontation and church discipline, but it all must be done in love and for the spiritual growth of the body of Christ in the earth.

---

1 Richard Ing, *Spiritual Warfare* (New Kensington, PA: Whitaker House, 1996), 30–31.
2 Ing, *Spiritual Warfare*, 44–45.

2

Witchcraft: Overcoming Witchcraft Attacks

This is a vital subject to cover in these last days for ministers. I would strongly encourage any minister to read *He Came to Set the Captives Free* by Rebecca Brown, *Deliver Us from Evil* by Cindy Jacobs, and *Listen To Me, Satan!* by Carlos Annacondia. There is a wealth of wisdom in these books. The subject of witchcraft is much broader than just spells, curses, and rituals. I want to take a moment to cover this.

SOME THINGS I SEE

Satan tried to kill all the babies in Moses' day, trying to get to Moses. He knew something was up and tried to prevent what God was doing. He also tried this same tactic when Jesus came into the world. Both times he was very unsuccessful. These last several years, satan has tried to wipe out a generation that has a very high call on it. He has used abortion to do the same thing he tried in the days of Moses and Jesus. But just as he missed Moses and Jesus, he has missed those God wanted in the earth today. There is a very high calling on the young people of our time. They will be the generation that sees the church in all its glory. They will see the unprecedented end-time revival and harvest. They will prepare the way for Jesus' second coming. The Lord is moving right now powerfully in preparing these young warriors. This is a time for children, youth, and college ministries to arise and be powerfully used of the Lord.

I don't know about you, but I want to be right on the cutting edge of what God is doing now, not years ago. I want to receive a fresh anointing today, not sit around talking about yesterday's anointing and yesterday's victories! Ministry to young people is what God is doing right now. Churches need to get into this flow. I believe one of the main purposes of the revival will be to equip these young warriors with such a high calling. I feel honored to serve them and be a father to them. Satan is also coming against this generation like no other. Sexual perversion is at an all-time high. It will continue to get worse.

One of the main ways satan has targeted this young generation is the rise of the occult and witchcraft in our time. Please understand that it does not bring glory to satan to teach on the occult and witchcraft. Rather, teaching on it exposes and defeats satan. The reason people are pulled into the occult is by curiosity. If it is exposed through teaching, the mystery of it is gone, and it loses its attraction. If there has ever been a time for the church to teach our young people the dangers of these things, it is now! Occult books sell like crazy in book stores. Young people are getting into witchcraft and wicca, thinking it is innocent, because no one is telling them any different.

Another thing I see is the deliverance ministry coming back to the church. Jubilee is an interesting principal in the Bible. Every 50 years, Jubilee would be decreed. Basically, each family had an inheritance, but because of hard times, a family might sell some of its property to another for the money. On the 49th year, the shofar would be blasted throughout Israel, and everything that God had originally given to a family would have to be restored unto them. Also, anything someone had that God had not originally given to them would be lost.

Satan has stolen so much from the church over the centuries. In the West we know very little of our Hebrew roots as Christians. Remember, we are engrafted into the olive tree of Israel. It's not the other way around. I would strongly encourage an in depth study on the tabernacle and the priesthood. Dick Rueben has some of the most incredible teachings on these things. He helped lay a foundation for the Brownsville Revival through these teachings as well.

Now back to what I was saying concerning Jubilee. The church was void of the baptism in the Holy Spirit at the turn of the 20th century. Satan had stolen it from the church. But the revival in Wales, led by Evan Roberts, was seeing souls saved and sparking hunger for a move of God all over the world.

William Seymour was a precious one-eyed black man who loved God with all his heart. He was going after God for a move of his Spirit. In a house on Bonnie Brae Street in Southern California, a revival of the baptism in the Holy Spirit broke out. People began to flock to this move of the Holy Spirit. Soon this handful of African Americans had outgrown the house and moved into an abandoned mission on Azusa Street. The great Azusa Street Revival had begun, and God used this mighty move of the Holy Spirit to bring Pentecost back to the church. All charismatic or Pentecostal churches have their roots in this move of God.

Fifty years later (we are talking about Jubilee), a great revival of healing came to America. Men of God like Oral Roberts came on the scene. God was restoring the healing ministry back to the church. Yes, there was always healing here and there, but now it was on television and a widespread scale. I sense in my spirit a move of God (50 years since the healing revivals of the 1950s) that is restoring the deliverance ministry back to the church. With the evil of the day is coming great bondage. People will be coming out of sexual perversions, occult practices, satanism, substance abuse, violence, having abortions, etc. They will desperately need to be walked through deliverance.

I feel this prophetically for ministers:

**We must prepare ourselves for this now so we will be ready.
Now is the time to study up on the deliverance ministry.**

Derek Prince laid the foundation through his two books *They Shall Expel Demons* and *Blessing or Curse: You Can Choose.*

WITCHCRAFT

Like a serpent, witchcraft has two fangs. Both are deadly. For many people who suffer snakebites, only one fang actually went into the skin. So with witchcraft, only one fang may be at work, but it is still witchcraft. If someone were to ask me for a simple definition of witchcraft, it would be "controlling others." One fang of witchcraft is controlling others in the flesh, and the other fang of witchcraft is using supernatural power to control others.

At the end of the age is the harvest (Revelation 14:14–20; Mark 4:26–29). All that has been sown in mankind, both good and evil, will come to maturity in these end times. Angels are assistants to true ministers. They can assist in the removal of hindrances to the purposes of God in these end times as well (Matthew 13:36–43). It is wise to always ask God to allow angels to assist in ministry endeavors.

Now dealing with witchcraft, Galatians 5:19–20 states, "The acts of the sinful nature [flesh] are obvious: sexual immorality, impurity and debauchery; idolatry and *witchcraft*." Witchcraft can be a work of the flesh. Have you ever known someone who tries to control people? They are either manipulating or intimidating.

For example, a husband feels it is not wise to get a new car right now. The wife withholds sex from her husband because she wants a new car. The old car runs fine, but she feels it is out of style. Her behavior is witchcraft. She is manipulating her husband to control him instead of submitting to his leadership. To submit means to *ask permission and obey the decision with a good attitude*.

One time, I heard a woman say, "I submit to my husband, but I do not obey him." She is a very confused individual. I know her, and she does have an issue with a Jezebel spirit. This is a common deception among those who do not like to submit.

In Ephesians 6:1 Paul commands children to "obey" their parents. This Greek word for obey is hupakouo. It literally means responding to commands with authority. It implies a forced obedience with punishment if not adhered to. And in Ephesians 5:22 Paul commands that a woman "submit" to her husband. The Greek word for submit is *hupotasso* in this passage. This word is translated "subordinate, obey, be subject unto." Even though the word means "to obey," it is not obedience demanded by the husband with punishment if not followed. The wife has a higher calling in that she willingly obeys thus submitting without being forced.

Because of the prevailing spirit over America, this part of scripture is neglected and twisted a great deal. Like it or not, it is the Bible. I do need to add that it is the husband's responsibility to lead. Many men in America don't lead especially in spiritual matters. Husband, listen to me, you will stand before God on judgement day and give an account for yourself, your wife, and your children. With leadership comes responsibility. You better be leading them into the purposes God has for them. Headship is for serving others, not lording it over them. Also, men are to love their wives as Christ loves the church. This implies a loving leadership, not a tyrant.

SUBMISSION TO AUTHORITY

I want to pause here and spend a moment explaining why God's way is best. In America the feminist movement (which is a Jezebel spirit's work) has made this message seem oppressive. In Genesis 3:15 God cursed satan and said, "I will put enmity between you and the woman." There is a special hatred satan has for women. Hands down, a woman is the most beautiful of all God's creation. Satan hates women because they bring life into the world, and he is the god of death! So God, in his wisdom, put a husband over a wife to protect her from satan. Then God went a step further and put a pastor over a family to protect them.

1 Corinthians 11 talks about a woman needing to have her head covered. This is a spiritual covering. It speaks of an authority figure like a husband or pastor to whom they are submitted. Notice I emphasized that the woman submits. There can be a pastor or husband, but if a woman is not submissive, she is just as vulnerable as if there wasn't one. Submission is for the protection of the woman. This covering is a sign of authority on the woman's head. That sign is like a "No Trespassing" sign to the devil. God intends for satan to have to go through a pastor then a husband to even touch the woman! Does that sound oppressive to you? It sounds like the work of a very loving heavenly father to me.

A woman might say, "That's easy for you to say; you are a man." Men have to submit to authority just like anyone else. Remember how Korah rebelled against Moses? God caused the earth to open beneath him, and he was sucked right down into hell (Numbers 16).

In 1 Corinthians 11:10 Paul says, "For this reason and *because of the angels,* a woman ought to have a sign of authority upon her head." The angels Paul is referring to are from Genesis 6 where fallen angels took wives unto themselves, had sex with them, and produced a race of beings called "Nephilim." Yes, that is in your Bible.

A woman who refuses to obey her husband opens herself up to a Jezebel spirit. This spirit attacks the woman's femininity. It will try to make her domineering and controlling. It will also attack her female organs with health problems like cancer. Jezebel is satan's direct attack against women. Women are protected from this through submission to male authority. I have three women in a group I am discipling right now. My goal is to see them in leadership, but I will not allow a woman in leadership who does not submit to her husband and to church leadership. If she is not submissive, she is not right with God and is wide open for satanic attack. She is not covered.

1. Manipulation, intimidation, and control: one fang of witchcraft

Not only can people be manipulating, but they can also be intimidating. Some people live causing others to be somewhat afraid of them. A man once said he could walk into a meeting with other men and get whatever he wanted. He goes in and intimidates all of them. They are afraid to say no to him. This is demon of "intimidation" or "fear" he operates under. It causes people to be paralyzed like a deer in headlights. They are gripped with fear to retaliate. So people use intimidation to control others. Have you ever known people like this? If you are a pastor, you have probably faced this in a board member. The way to deal with this is to go back to the seven steps to defeat Jezebel. This type of control is witchcraft of the flesh. Yes, there are demons involved, but the spells, curses, and rituals are not there. The individual is operating in witchcraft of the flesh. This is one fang of the serpent of witchcraft.

2. The magick arts: the other fang of witchcraft

The other fang is found in Revelation 21:8: "But the cowardly, the unbelieving, the vile, the murderers, the sexually immoral, *those who practice magic arts*, the idolaters and all liars—their place will be in the fiery lake of burning sulfur. This is the second death." I would take notice that in both Galatians 5:19 and Revelation 21:8 it says those who live like this will be in hell when they die. That is a scary statement. The magic arts are the working of spells, curses, or rituals to control other people usually through mind control. The use of witchcraft magic to control others is the other fang of witchcraft. This type of attack is usually in secret. You will feel the effect by experiencing either: illnesses, difficulty concentrating, confusion, fatigue, lethargy, depression, difficulty praying, or sudden events arising that hinder the purposes of God. Have you ever had these appear for seemingly no reason? Did the thought cross your mind that a coven was doing sacrifices against you and your family and cursing you? Well, let me promise you, if you are a minister, this is happening. That is why we must live holy! We cannot give an open door to the devil to really hurt us.

SATAN'S NETWORK

There is a tight network of world-ruling spirits, principalities, powers (Ephesians 6:10–16), lower-level demons, and those who serve satan (satanists). The more of a threat you become to satan, the more attack will ensue. If you are a threat of taking a city for Christ, you will face the principality over that city. If you begin to have world influence for Christ, you will face world rulers. Principalities carefully study a minister, his family and home life, and his strengths and weaknesses.

The word principality in the Greek is *arche*. We derive the word *architect* from this Greek root word. An architect makes blueprints to construct, then calls in the workers to actually carry out the work. These workers are known as "powers." We see that principalities and powers are usually seen in Scripture together. As a principality studies a man or woman of God, he lays out a carefully laid attack—a blueprint. Then when the timing is right, he will open the gates of hell and call up the powers to carry out the attack. The principality will usually get witches and covens to use their prayers and powers simultaneously with the attack to intensify its effectiveness. Blood sacrifices, especially human, greatly increase witchcraft power.

When this attack is underway, you better have on your armor and be ready. Evil spirits dwell in dark and dry places. If the light of truth comes, they flee. If the rivers of the Holy Spirit come, they flee. God desires for his people to have an open heaven over their lives, homes, and ministries. Deuteronomy 28:12 says, "The Lord will open the heavens, the storehouse of his bounty, to send rain [outpouring of the Holy Spirit] on your land in season and bless the works of your hands." What brings an open heaven is obedience to God's Word. What brings a closed heaven is disobedience to the Word of God. So principalities will also try to tempt a man of God in areas that he is weak. The purpose is to bring dryness by closing the heavens over his life through sin and disobedience.

Friend, I want to live in revival. I want to live so pure that the Holy Spirit wants to be around me. I want my home to be free from anything that would grieve the Holy Spirit so that the glory of God will rest there! When this happens, the glory becomes a canopy of protection. Isaiah 4:4–5 says, "The Lord will wash away the filth of the women of Zion; he will cleanse the bloodstains from Jerusalem by a spirit of judgment and a spirit of fire. Then the LORD will create over all of Mount Zion, and over those who assemble there a cloud of smoke by day and a glow of flaming fire by night; over all the glory will be a canopy." I want the principality in my area to see the glow of that fire when he sees my house! Isaiah says that after the cleansing, came the glory.

HOW IS YOUR HOME?

Let me ask you about your home. Is it a sterile place where it is hard to get along and hard to pray, or is it full of life and the presence of God? What makes a home sterile? Well, is there pornography, any occult materials or objects, anything connected with false religions, idols, or anything connected with Freemasonry? All of these things will allow demons in your home, and cause it to be dry, sterile, and absent of the glory.

Do you have things in your home that have control over you, like illegal drugs, alcohol, or tobacco products? Do you allow gossip, speaking evil of God's anointed, or strife in the home? Do you allow things across the television that have foul language, nudity, sex, witchcraft, or excessive violence? Demons can saddle the airwaves like we would saddle a horse and ride the waves right through your television screen into your home! Their feet hit your carpet, and they have come to stay. You now have a fight on your hands.

Do you demand honesty in your home? Do you go to bed angry with unresolved issues with your family? This will open a door to demons of strife, bitterness, etc. in your home. Do you have demonic or perverted music in your home? Do you have disorder? For example, do children obey parents, does the wife submit to the husband, and the husband take charge and lead the family in your home? I think you get the idea. These issues prevent the glory from coming in. I would suggest cleaning out your home, car, and life altogether from anything that would grieve the Holy Spirit. The Lord is looking for holiness in his people—especially his ministers.

After cleaning out your home, you can anoint the doorposts of rooms and speak blessings over every room of the house. Over the bedrooms, you can speak things regarding sweet rest and pleasant dreams. Over the living and dining rooms, you can speak blessings of sweet fellowship. Over the bedrooms and kitchen, you can speak blessings of health. There are some things that will bring the glory of God into a home. Anointing the home and speaking blessings definitely will. Let me name a few more.

Taking communion in your home will bring the glory in an awesome way. Listening to worship and praying in your home will bring the glory as well. One of the greatest ways to keep the glory is by keeping harmony in the home. Don't allow yourselves to go to bed angry with unresolved issues. Keep peace and harmony in the home. I have also heard of using the fruit of the vine from communion to apply to the doorpost of a home, thus applying the blood. This is also very powerful. We have a free download on our website regarding cleansing homes and land.

AN OPEN HEAVEN OR AN OPEN HELL

I was watching a Christian video on satanism and the occult. There was a brief clip from a service at the Church of Satan, started by Anton Lavey. Anton was carrying a sword and taking prayer requests of the people in attendance. He turned and called out, "May the gates of hell be opened wide," and then began to call up demons. The goal of satan is to have the heavens brass over an area and there be an open hell. Our goal is to see the gates of hell *closed* and heaven *opened* over an area. We have authority over all the works of satan and the gates of hell. Let's stand in our authority.

SATAN'S ATTACK AGAINST MINISTERS AND CHURCHES

I now want to discuss three main areas in which satanists and witches target ministers and churches. Please do not take these people lightly. Yes, we have more power and authority than them, but they can be very dangerous. I have been driving down the road and have been hit by an occult curse that almost caused me to black out and have a wreck. I discerned what was going on and broke the curse. I have had many other attacks like this that have affected my health or relationships around me or oppressed the ministry around me until they were broken. I have also felt as if I was spiritually suffocating until a breakthrough came. These attacks usually came before something new and powerful was released from the Lord into my life. Attacks always come before blessings. Occult curses do have some limited power. You will be wise to take them seriously. The three areas I want to discuss are direct attacks through witchcraft power (this chapter), infiltration of churches (chapter 3), and sexual attacks (chapter 4).

WITCHCRAFT POWER

I heard a story of a minister in a McDonald's. There was a woman near him, not eating. He simply made conversation by asking, "Are you not eating?" She replied, "No, I am fasting." The minister thought she was a Christian praying for something, so he asked her what she was praying for. "I am a witch," she said, "and I am praying and fasting that all ministers' marriages will be destroyed."

Well isn't that nice? By all accounts, her prayers have done well. The fact is that ministers are number one on these people's hit list. Let me assure you that the local coven knows your family, where you live, and your daily routine, and they are praying against you if you are really a man or woman of God. Don't be afraid. They have to go through Jesus to get to you, but we need to be aware of all of this. Even though Jesus could put us in a glass bubble, so to speak, and not let satan come near us, he doesn't do that. Jesus allows us to fight. He wants us to learn to fight—not to fight directly against people, but against world rulers, principalities, powers, and wickedness in the heavenlies (trying to make the heavens brass).

Witchcraft curses

Curses can be very oppressive even if we are living for God. Cindy Jacobs tells a story of how a Christian called her before she was to go minister. This Christian hurt her feelings. Well, she went to minister in a place where the spirit of death was very strong. She took a stand against that spirit. She later got home and felt herself dying. She knew she was dying. She cried out to her husband, who saw the situation. They quickly called prayer warriors to come to her aid. They discerned she had unforgiveness toward the Christian who hurt her feelings! This caused there to be a hole in her armor! So that spirit of death had an opening to attack her.

Are there any openings in your armor from unconfessed sin or unforgiveness? Don't be so quick to dismiss that without praying about it.

In another story, Cindy said she suddenly went completely numb on the left side of her body. A prayer warrior agreed with her. They discerned it was a witchcraft curse called "stun and numb." So they took authority over and broke it. She recovered instantly.

I have also heard stories of ministers being pushed down stairs by an unseen force.

Astral projection

Satanists can astral-project into homes and churches as well. They don't always send demons to do their bidding. Rebecca Brown does an incredible job explaining all this in her writings. So I won't go into astral projection too much. There have been many times I felt an evil presence come around me. I simply took authority over it, in Jesus' name, and it left. If it is stubborn about leaving, it is probably not a demon but an astral projected witch or warlock.

Ask God to release angels to remove them. He will.

WALKING IN WISDOM, NOT PRESUMPTION AND PRIDE

If you are out walking and see a satanic altar where there have been sacrifices made, it would be unwise to just presumptuously walk over and kick it over. It would be wise to make sure God is leading you to go kick it over, and that there are not holes in your armor. Do you have a powerful church you faithfully attend, and is there a strong prayer covering over you? Are you living holy? You better make sure before you do some of these things.

Be careful about touching satanic books and objects. Is God leading you to be handling these things? After touching all these things, I would pray for cleansing from the Lord. Touching these things brings defilement. These are cursed objects that have demons attached to them (Deuteronomy 7:26). There are times to touch these things, and we should certainly not be afraid to do so, but we must also use wisdom. If you are led by the Spirit into battle, that is one thing; however, some Christians move in pride and presumption. This opens them up to unnecessary battles God never intended for them to go through.

Deuteronomy 1 gives a great story of how Israel tried to go into battle when God was not with them, and they suffered a loss. Satanists will also try to place objects in minister's cars or on their property that will release curses. Be led by the Spirit in finding and removing these things. Henry Malone has a book called Portals to Cleansing. It teaches on how to cleanse land and homes, etc. I must say, it is a great book. In it he speaks of the power of claiming land for Jesus. Land can be cursed or blessed. That's why locations where murders have happened have an open hell and demons there. Unbelievers see these apparitions and think they are ghosts, but those of us that know the word know they are demons.

TAKING LAND FOR CHRIST

The Lord led me to a place in Dallas where those in witchcraft go regularly. I had felt led to pray over the land. When I got there, I could feel the power of satan in that place. The Lord had prompted me to take communion. After I took communion, the Lord prompted me to dig a small hole and place the bread in the ground and pour out the remaining juice, applying the blood of Jesus to that location. Some may not like this because it seems disrespectful to the Lord's supper. But it is not disrespectful at all. When I did this, I felt the power of that spirit break, and it lifted off that property very quickly. I had a friend with me who commented on the power of that moment.

Driving wooden stakes into boundary lines with scripture on them (setting spiritual boundaries and claiming land), the use of communion, and the use of anointing oil are all very powerful tools. Anointing oil can be poured out on land and rubbed on the doorpost of the rooms of houses. Communion is the most powerful in my opinion. The communion juice can be used much like anointing oil, and thus it will apply the blood (Exodus 12; Job 1:9–11). T. D. Jakes once said, "The battle is over land. Once you get the land, God will help you put whatever on it you need. But the battle is over the land." Once a location is cleansed of sin and the demons are driven off, a blessing should be spoken. One can lift their hands like a priest and say something like:

> The Lord bless you to be a sanctuary of rest and renewal. May you be a haven of peace where sounds of joy and laughter grace your walls and love and unconditional acceptance of one another is consistent in you. May God's presence dwell in you, etc.

THE INCREDIBLE POWER OF BLESSINGS

Look in the appendix for a list of blessings. There are times to pray over something and times to bless something or someone. Blessings are more powerful than curses and can cancel out curses. For example, a witch curses someone with sickness. A man of God, instead of praying, could place his hand on them and say, "May the Lord bless you with health in Jesus' name."

OUR MOUTHS: A LOADED GUN

We must be very careful what we allow out of our mouths. Words have so much power. Life and death are in the tongue. It is so powerful when parents will place blessings on their children. Blessings are basically speaking words by faith that are positive, and they are what you want to see come to pass in someone's life. But many parents will curse their children saying things like: "You are an embarrassment to the family. You will never amount to anything. If you keep on, you will be pregnant and in jail!" What a curse to put on someone.

Be careful, friend! God says we will give an account for every careless word that comes out of our mouths. Wouldn't it be powerful for a parent to pull their child up next to them and put their hands on them and begin to speak:

The Lord bless you with exaltation and promotion.

May you have a healthy and long life.

May your marriage and children be blessed.

May your home be a happy place.

May you have favor with God and man.

May you be successful in your workplace and be the head and not the tail.

May you live in prosperity and abundance.

May you walk in victory over your enemies.

This is simply an example of a blessing. You can write your own blessing. You can speak whatever you desire.

I know that pastors can bless congregations also. Basically, it is very powerful when someone in authority blesses someone under his authority.

If you have cursed people, places, or things, you need to ask forgiveness and break those words off whatever you cursed. Then replace the curses with blessings.

There are times to curse something. For example, you may pray for someone with cancer and say, "The Lord curse this cancer to dry up and die."

I have heard of a church cursing something like a pornographic store and it burning down over night.

There are times to pray, times to prophecy, and times to bless. We need to move with the Holy Spirit to know when to do what. John Kilpatrick has some incredible teaching tapes on this subject called "The Mystery and Power of a Blessing."

Many times, we complain in prayer instead of being thankful. We get negative with our words as we talk to family and friends. It's not long until we have cursed everything in our lives! It is important to guard our tongues.

BEING AWARE

Witches have made voodoo dolls of most ministers that are full of pins. I know this is not encouraging right now. Let me say, if you are truly living holy and in obedience to God, you are protected. You should never be afraid of satan. I am not afraid of satan, demons, or witches. What I am discussing has nothing to do with fear, but rather it has to do with wisdom. We need to know our enemy. I don't want to be unaware of his schemes. Satan uses people's fears and pride to control them.

If we are maturing in Christ, we should be growing daily in faith, humility, and love. The more we grow in faith and humility, thus dispelling fear and pride, the less control satan will have over us. Wheat and tares grow up together. The only way to tell them apart is at harvest time. The wheat has grain at the top that causes it to bow over because of its weight. The tares stand erect. Like the wheat, as we mature, we should be bowing over in humility more and more.

OUR INCREDIBLE AUTHORITY AS CHRISTIANS

Remember, we have dominion over satan. We are calling the shots in the earth as the church. We should have satan on the run, not the other way around. Satan should be afraid of us, not us of him. Take the offensive. Stay bold and strong in the Lord. Don't let satan intimidate you. A boxer that is on the offensive will be the one swinging, while his opponent is in a defensive posture, receiving the beating. We should be giving the devil the beating. So go into the land God has given you and take it for Christ. That principality has to bow to Jesus.

Let's now move into how satan uses satanists to infiltrate churches and destroy them.

3

Church Infiltration: How Satanists Infiltrate Churches to Destroy Them from Within

A friend of mine saw a man in church and was concerned. Having been around witchcraft in her past, she had a weird feeling around this man. He seemed spiritual and blended into the church. Even though this was true, she felt something wasn't right with this man. She sensed something evil about him. She had walked by him, and his face seemed to contort into the image of a snake around the eyes. It was as though something was leaping out at her.

During a service, this man would participate in the gifts of the Spirit, or so it seemed. One Sunday during morning worship, the power of the Holy Spirit came in very strong. She was sitting in the back watching this man the whole time. He began to squirm and was obviously very uncomfortable. A message in tongues was given, and the interpretation said something like, "There is a snake among the sheep." She watched as this man lowered himself all the way to the ground. He was literally lying on the floor on his stomach. She was shocked as he slithered like a snake to the back of the church. He then jumped up and ran out of the building and never returned.

This story is true and happened in a church near the Dallas area. It is very common for high-ranking satanists to attend churches—especially churches that are powerful. They attend to *destroy them*. It is also not uncommon for satanists to pastor churches, pretending to be Christian pastors. This requires tremendous discernment. I will list some ways those who serve satan enter churches and destroy them later. Right now, I want to discuss discernment.

WHAT IS DISCERNMENT?

The word *discernment* means "understanding." We use this term to mean "spiritual understanding." It is when an individual spiritually perceives what is going on in the realm of the spirit. They are able to look past the natural and perceive what is really going on, so to speak. Hebrews 5:14 says, "But solid food is for the mature, who by constant use have trained their senses to distinguish [or discern] good from evil."

Let me now say what discernment is not. It is not suspicion, criticism, or unrighteous judgment. These seem to be very apparent in the body of Christ right now. It never fails to irritate me to hear people credit satan with his little bit of power, but when it comes time to give glory to God for His power through His servants, they can't do that. Obviously, most of this is pride, but a lot is a lack of discernment.

I have heard many of my fellow teachers on deliverance and spiritual warfare give satan all kinds of credit for miraculous powers and strong attacks. This is very true. In fact, satan is also brilliant. These are all true facts, but he is nothing compared to God! When a man or woman of God rises up and God uses them to raise the dead or heal the sick, the same people will say the individual is doing that by the power of satan. Or they will question it. The Pharisees of Jesus' day did the same thing.

Matthew 12:22–26 says

Then they brought Jesus a demon-possessed man who was blind and mute, and Jesus healed him, so that he could both see and speak. All the people were astonished and said, "Could this be the son of David?"

But when the Pharisees heard this, they said, "It is only by Beelzebub, the prince of demons, that this fellow drives out demons."

Jesus knew their thoughts and said to them, "Every kingdom divided against itself will be ruined, and every city or household divided against itself will not stand. If Satan drives out Satan, he is divided against himself. How then can his kingdom stand?"

It is amazing how history repeats itself. I have read many books by Christian authors about spiritual warfare and deliverance. I have actually read one in which the author accused Benny Hinn of operating in witchcraft. How foolish. I usually don't read any more after that. If that individual has that little amount of discernment, why would I listen to him expound on spiritual things? I have heard others accuse Rodney Howard Browne of the same type of thing. Again, how foolish! Usually these people have never sat down and talked to them to hear their hearts, and they have never been to one of their meetings.

I want to say right now, those who are saying this are modern-day Pharisees and do not need to be followed or listened to. These false teachers may have "a form of godliness" (2 Timothy 3:5) but are denying God's power. These false teachers are suspicious. Many of them have given themselves over to demons of criticism, pride, and unrighteous judgment.

Being suspicious of everything that moves is not true discernment!

John Kilpatrick pastored one of the greatest moves of God in church history. His church hosted the Brownsville Revival. He tells a story of watching Christian television and being so critical of all that was on. He was driving his car one before revival broke out, and the Lord spoke to him, saying, "If you don't change, I will have to pass you by!" Being the man of God he is, he pulled over and repented of being critical of God's people. If you are critical of God's people, God will pass you by. This is not discernment! It causes division in the body of Christ and is very evil.

WHAT ABOUT MANIFESTATIONS?

Some people have a problem with manifestations of the Holy Spirit (falling down, shaking, speaking in tongues, etc.). These types of things are all throughout Scripture and all through church history. When we come into contact with the most awesome being in the universe, there will be manifestations. Something is going to happen! You don't put your finger into a light socket and nothing happen. I don't want to give too much time to this, because if someone is critical and not open, they won't receive no matter what you say.

Here are some examples in Scripture of manifestations:

- **Falling on the floor** (Ezekiel 1:28, 3:23; Daniel 10:9; Revelation 1:17; John 18:6; 2 Chronicles 5:14)

- **Shaking, jerking, or trembling** (Daniel 10:7; Habakkuk 3:16; Jeremiah 23:9)

- **Groaning and travailing** (Romans 8:26; Galatians 4:19)

- **Deep bowing** (Ezra 10:1; Psalm 35:13–14)

- **Heavy weeping and crying** (Nehemiah 1:4; Ezra 10:1; Joel 2:12)

- **Laughing** (Proverbs 17:22b; Psalm 126:1–3; Isaiah 61:3)

- **Dancing** (Psalm 149:3; 2 Samuel 6:16)

- **Being still and solemn** (Psalms 25:5; 27:14; 37:7; 131:2)

- **Being drunk in the Spirit** (Acts 2:13; Ephesians 5:18)

- **Having dreams and visions** (Acts 10:9–17; Joel 2:28)[1]

Pastor Kilpatrick was always a man of God who protected his sheep. He was open to God moving, but he had the wisdom to test the spirits to see if they are of God or not (1 John 4:4). There is a ditch on both sides of this. One can be so open to anything that they allow the demonic in, or one can be closed and quench the Holy Spirit. I am wide open to whatever God has. It may be different than the norm, but that is all right with me.

The current condition of the church scares me in this. People are so closed to God doing anything powerful and especially new, while accepting demons of criticism, pride, and unrighteous judgment that sow discord into the church.

Pastor Kilpatrick tells a story that before revival broke out in his church a man who had a strange spirit came to preach. The story goes like this:

> The year before revival came to Brownsville, an evangelist had called me. "There's a move of the Holy Spirit when I preach," he announced. I had already received reports from other churches where he held meetings. All reports seemed positive; people spoke of the Spirit's flow when he ministered. Hungry for revival, I had asked him to speak in a Sunday evening service. I am a cautious man. Before we went to the platform that night, I clearly stated, "Since I don't know you personally, I ask that when you are finished preaching, turn the service back to me. I can then lead the ministry time." The evangelist soon started to preach on revival. His sermon was sound and biblically based. Yet all was not well; a group of nearly 50 people had come with him, including the evangelist's teacher, and many who had sat under his ministry in other churches. Several sat on the front pew, with arms folded, staring at me while they punctuated the evangelist's sermon with shrieks of questionable laughter. Some stood up, only to fall to the floor. Their facial expressions and laughter troubled me. Now I have seen and heard people "laughing in the Spirit" and "falling in the Spirit" all my life. When it is from God, these expressions of the Holy Spirit are sweet and orderly. But this was different. I quickly sensed a "strange" spirit in some of these people, manufacturing fleshly manifestations. I was hungry for a genuine revival, not a carnal imitation. During several points of his sermon, I considered stopping the evangelist from continuing. However, in honor of God's Word being preached, I kept silent. Then the evangelist reached the end of his sermon. Instead of turning the service to me, he proclaimed, "Quick! If you want prayer, quickly come to the altar in front! Quick! I also need my catchers to come quick!" Before I could even get to the pulpit, he had already prayed for one woman who had come to the front, popping her on the head before she fell to the floor. I grabbed the microphone in hand and announced, "Ladies and gentlemen, this meeting is over. There's a strange spirit here tonight. I feel that the Holy Spirit has been grieved. This service is over."[2]

The pastor had the ushers sweep the aisles and take the group of 50 outside. When the group was escorted outside, some spoke of them throwing rocks at the church, revealing what spirit they were of. When Steve Hill came on Father's Day 1995, a true move of the Holy Spirit came that affected millions all over the world. Pastor Kilpatrick had discernment in all of this. He knew in his spirit what was of God and what wasn't. He had true discernment in that situation.

HISTORY REPEATS ITSELF

The great Azusa Street Revival at the turn of the 20th century had a similar impact in the earth. People would come from all over the world to be touched by the power of God and take the fire home with them. All Pentecostal and charismatic moves of our time can be traced back to Asuza. But while William Seymor was going after God with all his heart, there were critics of his day.

Have you ever heard of G. Campbell Morgan? He was a great Bible expositor. He was a man of influence. He stood back and said, "That is nothing more than the last vomit of satan!" How could a man of God say something like that! He missed God. We know that now, but he used his influence to deter many from this great move of God. He caused millions to end up in hell. Let me tell you how. Those who would have gone to Azusa would have been baptized in the Holy Spirit and gotten on fire for God. They would have led millions to Christ. People thought this man of influence must have known what he was talking about. He must have had discernment. No, friend, he didn't have a clue! He was a Pharisee of his day opposed to the move of God. It scares me how history is repeating itself today.

H. A. Ironside saw the manifestations of the Spirit at Azusa and said, "Insanities, worthy of a mad house!" You better be careful, friend. One day you could be in their shoes on judgment day.

Let me say this, because I know that some people out there have a problem with going somewhere to receive from God. How many times in the Bible did people go somewhere from their current location to receive from God?

I heard my pastor say, "I talked to a minister one time that had such a hard time with going somewhere to receive from God. I asked him if he had a sign in front of his church. He said yes. So I told him he better take it down, because he is asking people to leave where they are and come into his church to receive from God!" You see how ridiculous being opposed to going somewhere to receive from God really is! I personally believe that the only reason someone would have a problem going somewhere to receive from God is pride.

SEVEN TRUTHS THAT BRING SPIRITUAL DISCERNMENT

I am leading into how satanists infiltrate churches, but let me now go into how to have true discernment that is free from suspicion and criticism. Let me give you seven truths you can apply that will bring discernment.

1. It will not contradict Scripture.

Most people truly don't know the Word of God. This is from laziness. The Bible is full of the supernatural, and God is supernatural. Obviously, what he does will be as well. Read about life in the early church. It was full of signs, wonders, miracles, healings, angelic visitations, dreams, visions, thousands getting saved in one day, and strange happenings. I am convinced that if Jesus showed up in most churches, he would be kicked out.

If I were to spit on the ground and make mud that I put on a blind person's eyes, and I told them to wash in the bathroom sink, I would be persecuted by many—even though this is exactly what Jesus did in John 9:6. If I were to blow on someone during an altar service, I would be criticized like Benny Hinn has been, even though Jesus did this in John 20:21–22. This shows the condition of the church today. It is scary. Notice, I said it will not *contradict* Scripture.

What if God wants to do something new? Are you opposed to that? People would laugh during and after Rodney Howard Browne's meetings. He was criticized. I suppose those critics would have been happier if people left the meetings depressed. The problem was that it was new and didn't fit into their traditions. They are Pharisees—opposers to a move of God.

Even though Jesus and Elijah ascended into the air, I am sure if this sign happened in someone's meeting, people would cry witchcraft.

What if a minister had tens of thousands in front of him and knew he had to lay hands on someone in the back? Then God lifted him up and moved him to the back so he could lay hands on that person.

What if an evangelist were translated from Texas to Washington like Phillip the Evangelist in Scripture? Well, I am open to God. How about you?

2. The fruit of the Holy Spirit will be evident.

David Yongii Cho shares a story that happened in his church. He pastors thousands in South Korea, so it is not always that easy to discern everything that is going on at first. There was a woman who was prophesying. Dr. Cho does not have a problem with prophecy. In fact, he prophesied the Brownsville Revival would happen. He said, "A move of God will take place in Pensacola that will spread like fire across all of America." That is exactly what happened years later.

At any rate, this woman who was prophesying in his church had a line of people she was praying for during an altar time. He felt a check in his spirit about her. He noticed that she was somewhat rude when giving the words and that the words seemed negative. They came to pass, but something was not right. He went home to ask the Holy Spirit about her. The Holy Spirit spoke to Dr. Cho and said, "She is operating with a familiar spirit." A familiar spirit is an occult demon that gives information to people. It will attach to someone's life and feed them information like false prophecy. So Dr. Cho told her she could not prophesy in his church anymore.

Dr. Cho was not suspicious or critical, but he noticed a check in his spirit and that the fruit of the Spirit was not evident in this woman's life. A true man or woman of God will be loving, peaceful, full of joy, self-controlled in their lifestyle, living holy, good, patient, kind, gentle, and faithful. If these are absent, something is very wrong. Satan can give someone power, and accurate information, but he can never give anyone the fruit of the Spirit. This comes from the Holy Spirit alone. So don't let power or accurate predictions impress you. Instead, look at the fruit in someone's life.

3. They will have Christ's fruit in their ministry.

Jesus says, "He that does not gather with me scatters" (Luke 11:23). He also said, "You will know a tree by its fruit" (Matthew 7:15–23).

Some tried to speak out against the Brownsville Revival when it first broke out. People called the leaders of the revival false prophets, etc. Pretty soon, people realized the fruit. Thousands were getting right with God, healings were taking place, and a Bible school started that is sending people all over the world. The fruit of ministry began to be seen.

Are the works of satan being destroyed, and the works of Christ being manifested? This is a sign that God is at work.

4. Does your spirit bear witness it is of God?

Romans 8:16 says our spirit bears witness with God's Spirit that we are children of God. Also, Colossians 3:15 says, "Let the peace of Christ rule in your heart." The word *rule* there literally means be an umpire.

Above, I gave a story of an evangelist that came to Brownsville Assembly of God with a "strange spirit," and John Kilpatrick shut down the service. There is a part of the story I left out. Some of the members of his church left during the sermon and were in the foyer because their spirits were grieved at what they felt.

Let me ask you, is there peace in your spirit about it? That is an umpire to whether it is God or not.

5. What does the Holy Spirit say about it?

In the story above with Dr. Cho, the Holy Spirit said, "It was a familiar spirit." The early church knew to consult with the Holy Spirit about matters. In Acts 15:28 they wrote, "It seemed good to the Holy Spirit and to us."

Benny Hinn has some incredible teaching on the Holy Spirit in his books *Good Morning, Holy Spirit* and *The Anointing*. If you know the Bible, you will know when something is contrary. If you have an intimate relationship with the Holy Spirit, you will know when it is not him.

Finally, Paul wrote in 2 Corinthians 13:14, "The fellowship of the Holy Spirit be with you all." That word for "fellowship" implies intimacy. It is important to get to know the Holy Spirit intimately. It is vital in these last days.

6. Seek wise counsel.

The Bible says there is safety in a multitude of counsel (Proverbs

11:14; 15:22; 24:6). If you have concerns and need other opinions, seek out tested and true men and women of God and ask them. I would use wisdom about who I ask in these matters, especially if there are serious issues involved. Just as godly counsel brings safety, bad counsel could be deadly in some cases.

7. Listen to true prophets.

The Bible records that there are true prophets. These individuals have great vision and perception into spiritual matters. Many times, they will see past the veil of deception the enemy has erected. They will see the heart of someone and discern that the spirit that person has is not of God. I have heard stories and seen times when ministers ignored the true prophets to listen to the false, and the church greatly suffered because of it. Don't despise prophecy (1 Thessalonians 5:20).

SATANISTS IN CHURCH

Now let's get into how satan places his servants into churches to destroy them. This is very common, and if you are a pastor, you probably have this happening at least to some degree in your church. Many would think this would be easy to discern. Let me assure you it is not. How many would step out on a limb and say, "He is a satanist!"? The satanist could lie and say they are not, and the whole thing would backfire. Plus, there are Christians who are demonized and do foolish things, and they are not satanists. Also, satanists know the Word of God and Christian lingo. Satan has given them an evil anointing to do what they do, and they do it well. It will take a great deal of discernment to pick them out. You will also have to be wise in handling them, *but you do not want them in leadership, teaching, or laying hands on people!* That sounds obvious, but they are doing these very things in churches all across America right now.

I will draw a lot of information from Rebecca Brown's book *He Came to Set the Captives Free.* Chapter 17 of this book has incredible information concerning this subject. Elaine Lee was a very high-ranking satanist for years. She records being carefully trained and, in turn, trained others to infiltrate and destroy churches. The goal was to have churches become lukewarm and completely ineffective. It seems that satan has done fairly well in America. Satan had given satanists an eight-point attack plan. I will list the eight points as listed in Rebecca's book here:

1. "Establish a profession of faith."

Many satanists will come in and answer an altar call for salvation. They will weep and seem sincere. Also, they can very easily speak in a fake tongue by demons. Everything that is of God, satan will try to imitate. This can bring confusion, but we must not let it, by walking in discernment. The fake will cause many to reject the real or accept the fake. In Revelation 13:12–14 we see the false prophet bringing counterfeit signs and wonders to deceive the earth. For there to be a counterfeit, there has to be the real. Satanists will try to fake a profession of faith, but a satanist will not be able to look you in the eye and say out of their own mouth these words: "The Jesus who lived two thousand years ago, died, was raised from the dead, and is now seated at the right hand of God is my God." They can say, "Jesus is my God." But what "Jesus" exactly? I met a man named Jesus last week in Mexico. First John 4:1–3 will need to be applied here in this.

2. "Build credibility."

A person's credibility will come through faithful attendance, giving large sums of money, and being kind to people. They are always willing to help with any project, and they get to know the people of the church very well. This will help them find out who is real and who is not. They will use this to worm their way into leadership positions, and many are successful in this.

3. "Destroying the prayer base."

I would have to say this is one of the biggest goals of the satanist. Prayer is the key to power, protection, being in the flow of the Spirit, and revival. It should be one of the most important aspects of church, since Jesus Jesus said in Mark 11:17, "My house will be called a house of prayer to all nations." He put the emphasis on prayer! But most churches in America are too lazy for that type of commitment. Below is a true story of how a satanist infiltrated a church and destroyed it.

Notice how his attack was centered on destroying the prayer base of the church. Prayer and fasting are some of the greatest keys to revival.

The single most important goal of the satanists is to knock prayer out of the church. There are so many scriptures about prayer that we could not begin to list them all. A strong church is a praying church. Prayer requires self-discipline, and unfortunately, the majority of Christians spend very little time in prayer. Let me give you a true story of how a satanist destroyed the power of the very church in which I was delivered. Rebecca and I are brokenhearted over what happened, but we could not get the leaders of that church to listen to us.

Shortly after I was completely delivered, we were horrified to see that the high priest of the large and powerful coven of the city in which our home was located started attending our church. I knew the man and his family personally while I was still in Satanism, and he personally threatened both Rebecca and myself on more than one occasion. Within two short years, he and his coworkers completely destroyed this wonderful and powerful church! Many times, Rebecca and I pled in tears with the pastor and some of the elders to stop what was happening within the church, but they would not listen to us. We could not accuse "Roy" (not his real name) of being a satanist because it was our word against his. But we did try to show the pastor and a couple of the elders on more than one occasion that the fruits of his life were not scriptural. Here is what he did.

Roy was very wealthy. He joined the church shortly after he started attending it. He claimed to be well grounded and knowledgeable in the Scriptures, which he was. He contributed large sums to the church, attended every meeting and activity, and joined the choir. At that time our church had an extremely powerful prayer meeting every Wednesday night. Every week 200–300 people attended the prayer meeting and prayed as a unified body. We have been in prayer meetings so powerful that the power of the Holy Spirit literally shook the church building. These people were serious about prayer.

Then, as would be expected, the church began to experience tremendous growth. Its membership grew from 300 to over a thousand in less than a year. This is an exceedingly dangerous time for any church. The pastor and the elders were no longer able to know every member personally. Instead of dividing the church into a sister church to keep down the number of members to a manageable number, they built an addition onto the church, and the church kept on growing rapidly. Everyone thought they were being richly blessed by God—and so they were. But many of the newcomers were satanists posing as Christians.

Less than 6 months after joining the church, Roy stepped forward and told the church that God had put a great burden on his heart for America. He said that God wanted the men of the church to start coming once a week at noon to spend an hour in prayer for our country. He was willing to lead the group. Everyone thought this was wonderful, and Roy was much looked up to within the church. Within a couple of months he was made an elder, and shortly after that elected to the board of directors.

About 4 months after establishing the "Prayer for America" group, he launched his next two-pronged attack. He and his wife and about 20 choir members tearfully told the choir leader that they must stop attending choir because it "took too much time away from their families." They claimed that it was too much of a burden to have to attend the Wednesday night prayer meeting, then go to the choir practice after the prayer meeting. Needless to say, it didn't take long for the choir director to approach the elders about having choir practice *during* the prayer meeting, and "of course having their own prayer just before practice." The elder agreed and the 20 members rejoined. The first attack had been a success. Because the choir was large, a significant portion of the church members were now neither praying nor benefiting from those powerful prayer meetings. Most of the other church members began to wonder if the prayer meeting was so terribly important after all.

About a month after the victory with the choir, Roy attacked at a meeting of both the elders and board of directors. Roy told them that because of the fast rate of growth of the church that not enough time was being spent teaching individuals to grow in the Lord, or about how to share the gospel with others. He said that the Sunday schools just couldn't do the job. He also pointed out the fact that people did not know each other per-sonally as they used to when the church was smaller—all valid points. BUT his solution to the problem was to stop the large unified prayer group and split everyone up into small "disciple-ship groups" where they could be "individually taught" how to "grow and evangelize" and get to know one another better. The pastor, the elders, and the board of directors swallowed the bait hook, line, and sinker.

The prayer meeting was disbanded and small discipleship groups formed. Of course, Roy was in charge of forming the groups. The people he chose to lead them were mostly satanists. The prayer and the power of the church was destroyed.

Rebecca and I went to the pastor and some of the elders in tears, trying to show them scripturally that those powerful prayer meetings were the backbone of the church. They refused to listen to us. From each one we heard the same excuse. "Roy is the first one to know about the importance of prayer. Look how he started the 'pray for America group.'"

Many of the strongest Christians in the church shortly left and attended other churches. Within a year the church was in shambles. The pastor became discouraged and left the church, the older and strong members of the church left, and the power of that church was gone.

Do you see how easy it is? Is, or has, this happened within your own church? Don't just leave the church; please stand and fight satan. Put prayer back into your church.[3]

What a powerful story. I hope this shed some light on how satan uses these tactics all the time. The next point in the eight-plan attack is rumors.

4. "Rumors."

Many ministries and ministers have been devastated by rumors. So many Christians love to gossip and spread lies. I believe that judgment day will be very bad for them. If they make heaven their judgment will be severe, because they are a stumbling block to so many. A satanist can tell a bold-faced lie with no proof about a pastor, and many Christians will believe and spread it. Man of God, one word of advice: don't ever be alone with a woman! Many men of God have been set up and falsely accused this way.

5. "Teach and change doctrine."

Elaine says that she taught Sunday school in a large Bible believing charismatic church in her home town for several years, and led and taught the youth choir, while at the same time serving satan! She goes on to say that satanists will teach concerning three areas:

- Make prayer so difficult that no one would want to do it.

- Teach only health and wealth that will cause people to never want to suffer for Christ.

- Teach that Christians should never judge anyone (keeping satanists from being exposed).[4]

6. "Break up family units."

Satan wants divorce and strife in homes. One of the things that perpetuates this is having ministries for individuals and not families together. This can cause problems. For example, some churches *always* have the family divided at church with men's and women's ministries, youth, and children, etc. I love and believe in these ministries in balance, but if we never worship together, it can bring division in families and churches. Be wise and balanced in this! Satan can use it.

7. "Stop all accurate teaching about satan."

I have seen this at work. So many churches have a few people who will scream if you talk about the devil. They will say things like, "You're giving glory to satan!" How ridiculous! When we teach the Word of God that exposes satan, he loses power and influence. I believe Elaine is correct when she says, "Beware, the very church members who complain the loudest about any teaching about satan and his tactics will probably turn out to be satanists themselves."[5]

I want to say one more thing. If you are coming against some serious satanic opposition, you are going in the right direction! That is when satan will attack.

8. "Direct attacks by witchcraft against key members in the church."

We need to have intercessors who will keep the leadership and church in prayer. When I began a ministry in Dallas, the first thing I did was get those under me to commit to prayer. I believe if everyone will do their part, it will keep one or two from having to carry the load alone. I asked them to fast one meal a week and spend that time in prayer for the leadership and ministry. I even made a list of things to help them pray if they wanted to use it. We began and based our ministry on prayer. I also hold corporate prayer meetings. Also, there needs to be teaching on spiritual warfare. Your people need to learn to fight. When you start down this road, don't be surprised if you face satanic warfare on the way.

Even though the Bible never says only a minister that holds the office of a pastor has to be the one to oversee a church, traditionally that is what we have. Even some apostles, prophets, and teachers are called pastors if they oversee a church. There is nothing necessarily wrong with this, but I am making a point here. We all have different giftings and strengths. In these end times, those who oversee local churches must utilize what God has given them. I know Rick Joyner's church places people who have the gift of discernment as greeters, with ushers, in home cell groups, and in youth and children's departments to keep an eye on things. They are not there to be suspicious, critical, or judge by outward appearance, but rather to be sensitive to the Holy Spirit for anything that is not of God. Joyner says this has kept his church from many unnecessary difficulties.

We can be victorious in this kind of warfare if we will obey the Bible in testing the spirits and walk close to the Holy Spirit. I will reiterate that strong leadership is so necessary for the days ahead. Men and women need to not allow things in the church that should not be there. For example, in the story above, Elaine and Rebecca went to the leadership with concerns of how "Roy's" life was not lining up with Scripture. Why was he allowed in leadership with questionable character? This should not be allowed in the church. We must rise up and lead with authority in these last days. We must also stay in the flow of revival. The last day revival we are seeing is God's grace to the church in these last days. The Bible says, where sin abounds, grace all the more abounds (Romans 5:20). Let's put on our armor and press into the high calling of God for our lives.

1 John Kilpatrick, *Feast of Fire* (Pensacola, FL: John Kilpatrick, 1995), 100–104.

2 Kilpatrick, *Feast of Fire,* 88–89.

3 Rebecca Brown, *He Came to Set the Captives Free* (Chino, CA: Chick Publications, 1986), 238–241.

4 Lee, *He Came to Set the Captives Free,* 242–243.

5 Lee, *He Came to Set the Captives Free,* 245.

4

Sexual Attacks: How Satan Targets Ministers with Sex Magick and Seductive Women

I personally feel that this chapter is the main reason God has had me write this book. There is probably no other attack by satan that has been more successful than sexual attacks. The only other attack that could compare is the love of money.

DAVID'S STORY

Here is a story about David.

> He seemed to have the perfect life: a beautiful wife and a job that he loved. His church was bursting at the seams. David was frequently in the newspapers. Everything seemed to be coming together for David, except in his marriage. It had been months since he and his wife had been sexually intimate. Their marriage was becoming strained. He kept planning to take some time off from work.
>
> Then, David began noticing other women after seeing them in church, he would fantasize about them. One woman in particular caught his attention. He was pleased to see her name

scheduled in his calendar one day. Feeling more excited about seeing her than he should have been, he decided to guard his emotions cautiously.

The appointment went smoothly. The woman seemed vivacious and eager to serve. She secretly told David that her attractiveness had been a disadvantage in other churches. Two weeks later, she returned again. This time, she was wearing a full-length fur coat, which didn't seem strange at the time since it was beginning to turn cold outside. As she entered David's office, he closed the door, as was his usual practice since his secretary's desk was just outside. Standing in the middle of the room, the woman began to tell David how anointed he was.

She shared a vision of him preaching to kings and presidents, and she wanted to help him get there. She revealed that God had given her some insight. Looking into his eyes, she told him that she was aware he and his wife had not been intimate in a while. She knew his loneliness. Appealing to his pride, she said that David and other great men of this age were like "King David." Her role was to help the king in any way she could. Just as it was for David and Solomon, one woman could not satisfy the sexual needs of a man with such a great calling.

Intoxicated by her tantalizing words and sensuality, David stopped breathing for several seconds. Then in a bold move, the woman dropped her fur coat, revealing her nakedness. His heart pounding with anticipation, a powerful seduction came over him. Moving around the side of his desk, David touched her and gave into the craving that had gone unmet for so long. During the sleepless nights that followed, waves of shame and guilt washed over him. He wanted to run, to turn back the clock and erase what had happened. Eventually, David resigned from the ministry. His 3,000-seat building was later sold at an auction.[1]

THE PROTECTION OF MARRIAGE

How could such a thing happen to a man of God? Men of God need to be married unless God has given them a special grace to be single as the apostle Paul had. The Bible records in 1 Corinthians 7:5–7 for a husband and wife to not deprive each other sexually except for a time of fasting with *mutual consent*. Also, in verses 3–4 we read that a married man or woman's body is not his or her own. So the husband should fulfill his marital duty to his wife and likewise the wife to the husband. This means even if you don't feel like it, if the other wants sex, don't deprive them. That played a role in David's fall in the story above.

This woman was sent by satan. Just as there are satanist in every church to destroy the church, there are those sent to destroy the man or woman of God. Satan had targeted this man and knew his wife was not fulfilling her marital duty. Satan knew he was susceptible in this area. Now, I am not condoning the act. He still should have been faithful, but his wife's disobedience to the Bible played a role in this. Many men of God have been picked off by this attack. I will address this in a very detailed way later in this chapter. Let me give another story before going into some things.

KENNETH'S STORY

Here is another true story.

> Kenneth, who pastored a large church of several thousand members, was experiencing an unusual number of problems. Indecision plagued his leadership, unity among church members had begun to unravel, and the church had come under extreme financial hardship. A spirit of sickness and infirmity had begun to powerfully assault the intercessors and their families. It was the first time that such an unrelenting attack had come against the church. Even Kenneth's wife had become very ill.
>
> In the midst of these calamities, a "savior" appeared—a woman stepped forward to run the daily prayer meetings. At first, Kenneth viewed this woman as an answer from God, *despite the fact that two intercessory leaders warned him about this woman* [emphasis mine]. These intercessors claimed to have been given dreams and words of knowledge about this woman, which were hard for Kenneth to believe.
>
> Then, a church member, led by the Holy Spirit, happened to go to the new prayer leader's house. As she approached the door, she was startled by strange noises coming from inside. Concerned, she peeked in the front window. She was horrified

to find the woman kneeling on the floor, chanting, and sticking pins in dolls that were dressed like Kenneth's wife and other various church leaders. Later it was discovered that the woman was praying for the death of Kenneth's wife so that she could become his next wife.[2]

Man or woman of God, listen to me. Some of your most spiritual and discerning people are the prophets and intercessors. I know some in this field are flaky, but many are very solid and mature! Don't do as this pastor did and ignore the warnings from them! He could have prevented this attack. By giving this woman authority in the church, satan had legal right to bring this attack.

SATANISM AND SEX MAGICK

There are basically three types of rituals that are performed in satanism. They are described in the satanic bible written by Anton Lavey. The three rituals are the sex ritual, the compassion ritual, and the destruction ritual.

> The sex ritual is most commonly known as a love charm, or spell. A person casts this spell when he wants a new lover or to increase sexual desire. These rituals should not be taken lightly. I know of pastors in South America who have easily dismissed such spells and then fallen into sexual sin. One pastor, upon obtaining a vial of love potion, mockingly spread it on himself, only to later commit adultery.
>
> The Bible tells us of women who "hunt souls" with magic charms (see Ezekiel 13:18–20). A friend told me a story of a satanist whom she led to the Lord. He began to weep after his conversion and confessed that he had planted fetishes with spells in them in the yards of churches. His intent was to cause the pastors to fall into sexual sin.
>
> These fetishes will sometimes be made with graveyard dirt, urine and hair from private parts of the body. My friend went with him to dig up what he had planted. In each case, the pastor had indeed fallen into sexual sin.[3]

Let me give a warning to all who are reading this. There are men of God that have stood up behind pulpits and in pride said, "I will never fall into sexual sin like so and so." One man did this, and within a year fell into sexual sin. Pride comes before a fall, my friend. We need to pray for them and walk in humility. We also need a strong prayer covering for ourselves as ministers.

Basically, the compassion ritual is to receive a request from satan for yourself or a friend. The sex ritual is described above, and the destruction ritual will many times involve a voodoo doll. It is what we know as a curse or hex. It is meant to kill, maim, or in some way destroy someone. These rituals can have great power especially if the individuals using them are powerful in witchcraft and a sacrifice accompanies them. Shedding blood intensifies the power of a ritual. Human blood being shed is the most powerful of all.

WORDS FROM AN EX-SATANIST

I can't tell you the release it was to realize that I didn't have to do any more rituals, keep track of any more special days, always be aware of whether it was the full moon or new moon or a thousand other things. That's the basic difference between white witches or pagans, and the satanists. The satanists do blood sacrifices to appease the demons to get them to cooperate with them and give them power. The so-called white witches and pagans have to perform endless rituals to gain the same thing. AND they dress the demons up with fancy names and call them spirit entities or gods or energies or vibrations instead of demons.

Basically, satanists don't have the patience and discipline to spend so much time and effort performing meticulous rituals. It is much quicker and easier for them to do sacrifices. They gain the cooperation of more powerful demons that way. The others deal with the less powerful demons, but they are demons just the same, no matter what you call them. You learn very quickly in witchcraft that there are NO such things as impersonal energies. They are all VERY personal. You are either dealing with demons or the power of God, and humans cannot control the power of God. So anyone who is controlling an "energy" or "power" of any kind is dealing with demons. It is just that simple.[4]

SEDUCTIVE WOMEN: AN ARROW OF SATAN

To say that satanists target men of God sexually would be such an understatement. This is the first weapon that the enemy will try most of the time. It is very serious. What someone must understand is you are dealing with powerful demons. It is far more than just satan sending a pretty face. The enemy knows what you like and don't like. His servants will change their hair color, lose or gain weight, dress a certain way, change their personality, or do whatever it takes to seduce a man of God. These women are carefully trained in this. But it is much more than this level of manipulation. Then they will use sex magick to begin to send powerful sexual demons to arouse sexual desire in a man or woman of God. This can be a steady attack. It takes discernment to break this attack before it escalates. Fetishes planted in a yard open the gates of hell and release sexual demons against a man of God and his family. This can all put a man or woman of God into a stupor, so to speak.

NIGHTLY VISITORS

Something else the enemy will do is release sexual attacks at night. Nighttime is a time of great attack from satan. We are somewhat vulnerable while we are asleep. The enemy knows that. Satanists and witches meet at night. This is part of the reason. There are demons that take on the form of female (succubus) and male (incubus) sexual demons. Many men and women of God do not know what is happening to them. They will have very real, erotic, sexual dreams at night, and wake up feeling as though they literally had sex with someone. This is very real.

Also, a witch or warlock can astral-project into a home at night and take on this form as well. Astral projection is an occultist causing their spirit to leave their body and travel to a different location. When a witch or warlock is well practiced in this, it would be easy to travel to someone's home, in spirit form, to engage in sexual activity while they are at their residence in the body.

Some occultists claim that "astral sex" is extremely gratifying, since a woman or man could visit someone else without his or her knowledge and establish sexual contact. This type of contact is often called the incubus (male) or succubus (female) spirit.

Given what we know about astral travel, we cannot discount dreams that become extremely sexual. We might have been visited by someone in astral form.

This, of course, is the height of invasion of privacy and should never be done! If you are bothered by something like this, pray over your room before sleeping and ask the Lord to protect you with his angels. I have also found the reading of Psalm 91 out loud to be most helpful and protective.[5]

I have personally learned the power of taking communion before going to bed as well. When we consecrate ourselves under the blood of the Lamb of God, there is great protection.

A COUPLE OF STORIES FROM REBECCA BROWN

Rebecca Brown tells the following story in her book *Prepare for War*:

I was contacted by a pastor about John (not his real name). John was a young man in his twenties. He had been a regular and enthusiastic attender of this pastor's church for about five years. This church practiced deliverance and had a vigorous street ministry. John spent many evenings witnessing for Jesus Christ to people out on the streets. He often took people into his home who needed help. His wife was a Christian also and worked with John in the Lord's service.

All went well until one day John took a man into his home for help whom he thought was a Christian. As it turned out, this man (whom I will call Mike) was a satanist. One night, he overcame John, hypnotized him and began demonically controlling both John and his wife. Within two weeks their marriage was in a shamble and John and his wife were ready to separate. They sought the pastor's help, and were finally able to recognize the source of their problems. John immediately made Mike move out and leave his home. Both he and his wife received deliverance from the many demons placed into them by Mike through hypnotism.

Unfortunately, John's troubles did not end there. Shortly afterward, he awakened every night from his sleep screaming. He said that, although he could not see him, he knew Mike was present in the room. The invisible Mike would pin John down on the bed and sodomize him. John had never participated in any sort of homosexuality at any time in his life, and his horror at what was happening to him threw him into a panic. Although he could see nothing, he clearly felt his rectum being penetrated as if someone was physically committing the act.

This occurred over and over again. John was a nervous wreck and exhausted from lack of sleep. He and his pastor anointed his house repeatedly. They went through everything in the house looking for any possible object left there by Mike. Finally, John and his wife moved. Nothing helped. This was when they contacted me.

I had several long talks with John and his pastor, looking for the key. I knew that since anointing the house did not succeed in keeping Mike's astral projected spirit out, that either the Lord was permitting this battle for some reason, or most likely, there was some legal ground for satan in John's life.

We spent several frustrating weeks searching for the key. Finally, after much prayer, I was lead to ask John more about his parents. John is an American Indian. He did not know much about his parents because he was raised in a foster home. But he did know that his father was a "Shaman" (witch doctor) of the tribe and had heard that he was skilled in "shape changing." This was the key. John had inherited a demonic link between his soul and spirit from his parents. It had remained unnoticed until Mike came to live with John. The demons in Mike told them about the link, and I have no doubt that through the hypnosis, Mike placed demons into John to control this link. This is how Mike could astral project into John's bedroom and engage in homosexual activity with him. Because of the inherited link, John felt everything.

As soon as John renounced his inheritance and asked the Lord to sever between his soul and spirit and to cleanse his spirit completely, the attacks stopped.

Here is another story from *Prepare for War*.

Kerry (not her real name) is a young lady who became involved in Satanism at the age of 15. She became sexually involved with many demons and also with the high priest. By the time she was 20, she could no longer deal with the emptiness she felt, and she accepted Jesus as her Savior and Lord. She received deliverance from many demons, but the next two years were filled with torment. Night after night, both the high priest and demons returned to rape her. She tried to rebuke them but was unsuccessful. Finally, she got into contact with me. The people who had helped her get rid of many of the demons did not know they needed to clear out her spirit or that she should ask the Lord to sever between her soul and spirit.

Once she did this, most of the torment stopped. However, the demons still returned to try to rape her, suddenly throwing her down onto the floor. Once she had asked the Lord to sever between her soul and spirit, she could no longer "see" the demons. And, since they no longer had legal ground in her life, they had to leave when she rebuked them in the name of Jesus. They were no longer successful in their attempts to rape Kerry, and, over a period of several months as she stood firm in the Lord, the battle lessened. After a year or so, she was no longer bothered with those particular attacks.[6]

These stories may seem a bit strange to someone who has never been in witchcraft and never prayed for deliverance of those who are coming out of it, but we must be ready for these precious people. What if this story above was your daughter that had rebelled and served satan. What love would you show her?

PROTECTION FROM ASTRAL PROJECTION

Elaine Lee gives this encouraging story of how God will protect his people from astral projection by angels. She writes:

It was during that last visit to California that one of the incidents happened that started me questioning satan's claim to being more powerful than God. The high priest gathered a number of us together and told us that there was a family nearby who had been interfering with satan. They had been converting a number of the cult members to the enemy, Jesus Christ, and were making a nuisance of themselves. Satan had given the order for them all to be killed. The high priest told us that we were all to go together in our spirit bodies (astral project), and kill them. So, we sat down in a circle with our candles in front of us and consciously left our bodies going in our spirits to the house to destroy these people. I was not at all enthusiastic about the project, but I had no choice. If I had disobeyed I would have been killed.

Much to our surprise, as we arrived at the edge of this family's property, we could go no further. The whole area was surrounded by huge angels. The angels stood side by side holding hands. They were dressed in long white robes and stood so close together that their shoulders touched. They had no armor or weapons. Nobody could get through them, no matter how we tried. Any kind of weapon used merely bounced off of them doing them no harm. They laughed at us at first, daring us to come ahead and try to get through them. The other cult members got more and more furious with each passing moment. Suddenly their eyes made all of us fall backwards onto the ground. A very humbling experience, I might add!

I will never forget—as I sat on the ground looking up at them, one of the angels looked directly into my eyes and said to me in the most loving voice I had ever heard, "Won't you please accept Jesus as Lord? If you pursue the course you are taking you will be destroyed. Satan really hates you, but Jesus loves you so much that He died for you. Please consider turning your life over to Jesus." That was the end of the battle for me. I refused to try any longer to get through. I was very shaken. The others tried for awhile longer, but none succeeded. I doubt the family ever knew of the battle going on outside their house. They were completely protected! We called this particular type of special angels "link angels." Absolutely nothing can get through them. I was secretly thankful we didn't get through and the link angels had given me much to think about.[7]

DOREEN IRVINE'S TESTIMONY

The fact that we need compassion for those who need deliverance reminds me of Doreen Irvine's testimony. She wrote a book of her testimony entitled *Freed from Witchcraft*. It is an incredible book. She was raised by an abusive alcoholic father, then ran away and lived on the streets. She became a prostitute, stripper, and heroin addict. During one of her nights of stripping, she overheard some ladies talking about a satanic church. So she asked them if she could go. They blindfolded her and took her to a satanic church. She gave her life to satan and began to participate in all the rituals. The High Priest became her lover. He led her deeper into black magick witchcraft. She could make herself become invisible or kill animals by simply looking at them. She was the High Priestess of a coven of witches.

She heard of an evangelist coming to town and hated him without reason. It was obviously the demons in her. She was so tired of serving satan that she went to one of his meetings and gave her life to Christ. Well, they told her they were leaving town and she needed to start going to church. So she did. She went to several churches, but when they would mention the blood of Jesus or take communion, she would manifest demons and slither around on the ground, scream, or run out of the meeting. The religious people of those churches looked down their noses at her. She never got help. So she went to another church.

After service she was leaving, and the bishop asked her if there was anything they could do for her. She said, "Yes, I am addicted to heroin and have come out of satanism and witchcraft. I need help." She said the bishop turned as white as a sheet and said, "Well, I wish you well. Come back and see us." Out of sheer desperation she cried out to God. A man approached her on the street and gave her a phone number to a minister who could help her. He was truly a man of God who was not afraid of demons. He met with her and drove out the demons, and now she is a trophy of God's love and grace.

Are you ready to help these? I would advise you to get that way.

ANOTHER YOUNG WOMAN'S TESTIMONY

John Kilpatrick tells this story in his book *When the Heavens are Brass:*

For three weekends in a row, a striking blonde woman walked into the service with a couple I had never seen before. Even though the three were visibly touched by the Spirit of God during the services, they didn't come down to receive Christ. I wanted to meet them, but they left so quickly after each service that I just couldn't reach them in time. They vanished after the third Sunday, and I turned my thoughts toward the ongoing ministry at the church.

Several months later, on the exact day I had finished a 13-day fast, my executive assistant, Rose Compton, knocked on my office door and said, "Pastor, we have an emergency out here. Do you have a few moments to see this lady?" I knew by the look on Rose's face that something was seriously wrong, so I told her to bring the lady in.

When the woman entered my office, I was appalled by the look of death I saw on her face. Her face was ashen-gray, her blonde hair was unkempt and in disarray, her sunken eyes were dull and red-rimmed, and it was clear she was in torment. I knew I had never met her before, but there was something familiar about her appearance. Then I remembered her: This was the blonde woman who had come to the Sunday services months before! Now I barely recognized her.

After Rose introduced the visitor, I said, "I think I remember you from some of our Sunday services. Didn't you come a while back with a redheaded woman and her husband?"

"Yes, pastor, that was me. I just wish I had never left."

"What happened to you? Are you okay?"

The young woman's eyes filled with tears. She told me that one rainy night weeks after she had stopped coming to our church, she was driving along a deserted stretch of highway when she saw a young woman walking alone beside the road. She felt sorry for the woman, so she stopped and offered her a ride. She ended up taking the hitchhiker home, where she fed her, got her some dry clothes, and tried to comfort her.

The young woman in my office looked down for a moment, then said, "I don't know how it happened. I've never had any thoughts or desires in this direction, but somehow she seduced me, and we ended up in bed together in a lesbian relationship." This woman had been a virgin up until that time, but the hitch-hiker managed to manipulate the young woman's well-meaning desire to comfort and help. She looked up at me in her shame and said, "I'll never forget what she said when it was over. As she left the room, she looked back at me and said, 'Oh, by the way, I'm a witch.' Something sinister immediately crept over me."

From that night on, the woman's life quickly fell apart. By allowing herself to be seduced into having lesbian relations with the witch, she had opened up her life to demonic oppression.

Evil spirits began to come at her right through her bedroom wall in the middle of the night. The near constant torment made her unable to sleep. Then she lost her appetite. Finally, she began to lose any desire or ability to take care of herself.

The enemy realized that this young woman was almost ready to receive Christ after her visits to the church, so he ordered a principality, an architect of evil, to hatch a plan and lay a trap. He connived to make the heavens over her head brass. As a result, this woman nearly lost her soul, and possibly her life.[8]

Brother Kilpatrick was able to help this woman get back to where she needed to be with the Lord. I encourage you to learn how to minister to these people.

So how did this woman who had never had a homosexual tendency in her life end up sleeping with the hitchhiker? How do great men of God fall prey to having sex with a woman, only later to lose everything, and live to regret it? As people of God we cannot afford to be unaware of satan's schemes.

QUOTES BY ANTON LAVEY

Sex magick is a powerful tool for those who serve satan to use against us. I am putting some direct quotes from Anton Lavey, who wrote a book called *The Satanic Witch*. In this book he teaches women how to seduce men sexually. He says that if you can find what a man likes sexually, you have got him. The reason I am putting this information into this book is because it is what I am talking about with sex magick. It must be taken seriously. *Also remember the stories above as you read this.* You may want to ask God to cleanse your mind of any defilement after reading it.

On Teaching Women to Entrap Men through Sex Magick

Most women know the old trick of unbuttoning one of the middle buttons of a blouse so that it will appear as though it accidentally became unfastened. This is always good for a sneaky peak at what lies beneath as you move about. In utilizing the Law of the Forbidden, you can make many of the things you do appear as though you were unaware of them happening. Thus, you will be employing a double threat by your proper and conducive choice of garments and also by your apparent lack of knowledge of your exposure.

The only thing you must realize, when performing little rituals, is sexual self- consciousness. It is the positive value of such an experience. That here can be a secret thrill connected with each exercise there is little doubt. What is important, however, is that you make a ritual of the experience.

A ritual is an act, or series of acts, that are entered into with complete and total awareness of one's actions, plans, feelings, and purpose. All rituals do not take place in a specially designed chamber as you shall see. If you want to be a witch, you'd best learn the first three dimensions before you concern yourself with the fourth. The only way to start is to become aware of your own existence—super aware! Then, in what will appear to be the most subtle and non-esoteric ways, make others who will increase your witch-power aware of your existence.

Because sexual energy is potential magical energy and nature intended that they be attracted to you, men are your best source of witch power. Therefore, by your own sexual self-consciousness, you can draw this power from the men who need only to be placed within your magnetic field. Remember, the purpose of a ritual such as the one I'm about to describe is not to pick up men but to produce within yourself an accelerated charge of sexual self-consciousness.

While performing your ritual, remain as aware as possible that you are doing something naughty, forbidden, possibly even nasty. This is not the time to try to scrape your psyche clean with thoughts of breaking inhibitions and false guilts. This is the time to turn unfounded guilts and inhibitions into an advantage! Allow yourself to feel as self-conscious as you can.

The Sex Ritual

Apply your makeup so you feel as though you look as seductive as possible. Fix your hair in an attractive manner. Take off all your clothes and step into the sexiest pair of high-heels you own. Now you are glamorously decked out at your highest and lowest extremities, head to toe. Go to your closet and get your coat, *only your coat,* and put it on and button it. Now go out.

Go where there will be people, especially men. If you are driving, stop in a gas station to use the rest room, so the attendants can see you. Go into a newsstand for a pack of cigarettes, where men are playing the pinball machines. Walk around.[9]

Does this remind you of the first story I wrote in this chapter? The woman came into the pastor's office with nothing more than a winter coat on. The pastor literally was mesmerized as she spoke to him. She had him under her spell!

Anton Lavey also stated that if a woman can get a man to masturbate while thinking of her, he has performed a magical act with her. This act increases her power as a witch. The goal this woman has is to get as many people to lust after her as possible. Demons feed on sin. This causes her sexual demons to grow more and more powerful. She will have demons of lust and seduction that cause a spiritual pull that draws men to her sexually. The ritual is not over.

As soon as you get in your room, remove your coat and stand before the mirror. Imagine that you see yourself as a desirable man would see you, perhaps one you encountered during your walk. Look at yourself from an imaginary man's body, allowing yourself to feel as sexually excited as you would if you were a man.[10]

While looking in the mirror, he encourages the woman to masturbate and reach a climax while thinking of a certain man. (I am editing this tremendously.)

I know that this is not the easiest thing to read (or to write, for that matter). But in the day we are living in, this information can help ministers be aware of satanic warfare on this level. If this writing helps to keep one man of God from falling into sexual sin, it is worth it all. Please pray for all your spiritual leaders. They are under more of an attack than many realize.

I will fast-forward to another part of the ritual that concerns nightly visitations. These women who practice sex magick are known as sex-vampires. They draw off the sexuality of men. Lust causes them to grow in power as a witch. Anton goes on to say about them:

When you resume your normal activities, after getting dressed, you have symbolically closed your ritual chamber behind you. The combination of all the elements we have discussed cannot help but have an accumulative side-effect in the awareness you have of your own powers of seduction and the *aura which will surround you* [empasis mine].[11]

Some women carry a lustful presence about them. When sex rituals like this are performed toward a man of God, it releases powerful demons to begin to (1) arouse sexual desire from within the man or woman of God, (2) cause lustful thoughts in the mind, (3) begin to tempt him/her sexually, (4) or possibly cause strong sexual attraction toward the witch or warlock that is sending the spell. Watch out, men and women of God!

There was a church here in the Southern states in which a young pastor fell into sexual sin with multiple women. Back in those days, the parsonage was attached to the church. Sadly, the church leaders had to tell the wife and children he was unfaithful so that they had to move out for the new pastor, and his family, who would be moving in. The leaders helped pay for her to move back to her parents' house. Anyway, this new pastor comes in and begins to be tormented by sexual dreams and lusts he has never felt before. He tells his wife about what is going on. She contacted several powerful intercessors she knew. They all went to the church and began to pray and anoint that church and parsonage and drive out everything defiled and demonic. All the lusts and bad dreams disappeared. That church began to grow and experience revival after that cleansing.

In this next ritual I will record, "How to Become a Succubus and Attack the Man of Your Choice While He Sleeps," Anton Lavey teaches women how to astral-project themselves to a man and sexually seduce him. In this way, they actually become the succubus spirit themselves.

"How to Become a Succubus and Attack the Man of Your Choice While He Sleeps"

A succubus is an evil female demon who visits men in the night and, while they are sleeping, has sexual intercourse with them. All you need is an indelible image of his physical attributes in your mind, a burning lust, a place to work it out, and some help from other men. Choose a time when he has been asleep for at least four hours. Exercise your sensuality by going forth earlier in a manner to excite other men, even if only visually, employing the Law of the Forbidden the Virtues of Embarrassment. Do not depend upon your strong desire for the man you wish to summon, as it alone is not enough. It is important that you engender the lust-energy from other men, as they will be supplying, through their sexual fantasies of you this night, the proper balance—the completed circuit of needed energy.

Enter your chamber at the prescribed hour and start to masturbate. If you can force his image into your mind at climax, it is highly likely he will receive your visitation. If a man who is masturbating with your image in his mind or who is having intercourse with you should reach climax, and at that time you envision the object of your desire and you yourself reach a climax while thinking of your quarry, you will be sure to reach him as he sleeps.

If you wish, add some incantations or burn some incense or candles to make your charm more "magical".

As a succubus, the purpose of your working is to enter his mind and body as he sleeps, although such things often prohibit sleep.[12]

These are the writings of a satanist who had obviously completely given himself over to sexual demons. This is what satanists are teaching their women. You take this powerful magic, add a good-looking woman, put her in a church where she appears spiritual, and this can be a deadly combination for some men out there. The fact that a man of God might be having marital problems only makes the situation even more deadly. Satan has a way of sending these women during a time a man is going through marital problems. This type of thing is happening all the time. I talk to other men of God who confirm to me that they have experienced these attacks at night. They had no idea what was really going on. By exposing satan in this way, he loses power. Please pray for ministers, because there is an intensified level of warfare we face.

WARNING FROM THE HOLY SPIRIT

I would strongly encourage anyone who feels a call to ministry to set aside a time of prayer and fasting in which they ask God to show them and deliver them from any work of satan or an open door that could make them vulnerable to the enemy.

Some men out there know that they have a strong weakness here. Prayer and fasting can break through this. You may also want to go to a ministry that specializes in deliverance to make sure all doors are closed to satan. *I believe it will be vital in the days ahead that ministers have no open doors to satan.*

In the next chapter, I will walk you through some basic teaching on the subject of deliverance.

1 John Paul Jackson, *Unmasking the Jezebel Spirit* (North Sutton, NH: Streams Publications, 2002), 92–93.

2 Jackson, *Unmasking the Jezebel Spirit*, 99–100.

3 Cindy Jacobs, *Deliver Us from Evil* (Ventura, CA: Regal Books, 2001), 144–145.

4 Rebecca Brown, *Becoming a Vessel of Honor* (New Kensington, PA: Whitaker House, 1990), 38–39.

5 Jacobs, *Deliver Us from Evil*, 131.

6 Rebecca Brown, *Prepare for War* (New Kensington, PA: Whitaker House, 1992), 272–273.

7 Rebecca Brown, *He Came to Set the Captives Free* (Chino, CA: Chick Publications, 1986), 56–57.

8 John Kilpatrick, *When the Heavens Are Brass* (Shippensburg, PA: Revival Press, 1997), 51–52.

9 Anton Szandor LaVey, *The Satanic Witch* (Los Angeles, CA: Feral House, 2003), 235–239.

10 LaVey, *The Satanic Witch*, 240–243.

11 LaVey, *The Satanic Witch*, 240–243.

12 LaVey, *The Satanic Witch*, 250–252.

5

Deliverance: Breaking through Every Stronghold

I heard a great man of God make this statement in a sermon one time. He said, "We must pull down every stronghold and move into the last-day anointing!" If, in reading this book, you have felt tremendous oppression, have battled illnesses, had abnormally strong sexual arousal (by reading the previous chapter), or strong confusion or lethargy hit you, this could indicate that there may still be some open doors to the enemy that need to be shut. A stronghold is a place satan has dominion.

SIGNS OF DEMONIZATION

Here are some signs that someone has demons at work in their life: Fits of rage, constant headaches, insomnia, incurable diseases, fears, mental illness, seizures, suicidal thoughts, female problems, depression, addictions, fascination with the occult, lust, nightmares, hearing voices, seeing scary visions, stubborn arrogance, compulsive lying, stealing, or dishonesty, marital problems, dizziness or fainting, or sharp unexplained pains in various parts of the body.

PAVING THE WAY FOR DELIVERANCE

The prayer below can begin the process of deliverance, but it will take prayer, fasting, and deliverance to truly see all doors shut. You can pray this prayer *out loud* to begin the process:

> Father, you promised in your Word that all who call on your name will be delivered. Therefore, I ask you to show any areas that need your deliverance. Reveal them to your servant that I might not be vulnerable to the enemy.
>
> I ask you to cleanse me from all my past. I confess and repent of all my sins, transgressions, and iniquity in my life and those of my ancestors. I ask you to wash away all sin, blot out all transgressions, and take all iniquity out of me and my family by the power of the blood of Jesus.
>
> I renounce satan, his works, and his kingdom. I renounce all occult practices, false gods, false religions, and idolatry. I formally renounce any oath, pledge, prayer to an idol, or dedication to a false god that was obviously not of you. I renounce sexual immorality or any violence or shedding of innocent blood.
>
> I pledge my life and family to Jesus Christ alone. I dedicate my family and descendants to Jesus and cover them in his blood.
>
> I ask you to show me anyone I have unforgiveness toward. As an act of my will, I choose to forgive_____ though I may still be hurt and angry by what they have done. I thank you for healing me from the hurt that I may love them the way you do.
>
> Any demons that have had access to my life because of these things, I serve notice that your legal ground is cancelled and command you to leave now, in Jesus' name!

All this prayer has done is pave the way for deliverance. There may be generational curses that need to be broken, soul ties that need to be broken, words or prayers that need to be broken off your life from someone who sent them, or curses, spells, or rituals from witchcraft that need to be broken. All of these things will have demons at work that have been empowered by them. Let me walk you through some of this.

GENERATIONAL INIQUITY AND CURSES

I don't like the words demon possessed, which implies ownership, in describing Christians with demons. For example, I own a silver ring. I can destroy it because it belongs to me and is my property. As

Christians, we are Jesus' property, but I do believe that Christians can be *demonized* (under the influence of demons) and have legal ground for demons to bring destruction into their lives. I have personally cast demons out of many Christians. I have had Christians I prayed for who had demons speak through their vocal cords, their face contorted to look like a snake or cat, or thrashed about on the ground, screaming as demons came out of them. This may not fit into your theology, but maybe we need to reevaluate some of our teaching. When Jesus came, He came to God's people. These were the Jewish people of His time. He drove demons out of *God's covenant people.*

Secondly, God's people can have open doors for demons to enter their lives and steal, kill, and destroy. This leads me to the fact that most of us have to deal with generational curses unless we have come from a powerful Christian lineage going back several generations. How many of us can say that? We all have around 30 people who directly affect our bloodline going back four generations. Can we safely say all of them never were involved in the occult or sinned in a way that released a curse on the family? Exodus 20:3–6 shows a curse released to the third or fourth generation of those who worship other gods and a generational blessing to a thousand generation of those who worship only the Lord.

A generational curse works like this: If an ancestor was involved in the occult, idolatry, a false god or religion, Freemasonry, etc., that sin caused a curse. The curse has released demons that are now at work in the family line. This will cause either poverty and major financial difficulties, mental illness in the family line (including depression or nervous breakdowns), physical illnesses that travel in the family, or family strife, divorce, and alienation.

Do you see these things in your family? I have American Indian ancestry (they operate in witchcraft) on one side of the family and Freemasonry on the other! I had two curses to break. When they were broken, the family's finances dramatically improved, health improved, and a love and closeness came in relationships. Derek Prince gives seven indications there is a curse in a family line in his book *Blessings or Curses: You Can Choose.* Here they are:

1. History of mental or physical breakdown

2. Repeated chronic sickness (from one sickness to the next)

3. Barrenness or a tendency to miscarry

4. Divorce or family alienation

5. Continual financial stress or poverty

6. Accident prone (repeated unexplained accidents)

7. History of suicide or early deaths

Do you see any of these, or a combination of these, in your family? Sin means "missing the mark." It implies something done that was wrong, but not with premeditation. Transgression, on the other hand, means "rebellion." It implies a premeditated rebellion against God. In other words, someone knows the act is wrong but does it anyway. Iniquity is altogether different. It means "bent, crooked, or perverted." Iniquity is something that is within someone, passed down the family line, that produces a weakness to a certain sin.

For example, there could be a tendency toward alcoholism, anger or abuse, draw toward the occult, controlling behavior, or strong sexual perversions. These weaknesses travel down the family line and even though someone does not want to do these things there seems to be a weakness toward them and they end up becoming just like their father, for example. This cycle of iniquity can be broken by asking God to forgive and remove it. Cindy Jacobs does a fabulous job explaining this.

> The biggest open door to curses is generational iniquities. Generational iniquities are an open door to generational curses that have been passed down through the family bloodline. The Bible refers to these in a number of places, including Exodus 20:5:
>
> "You shall not bow down to them nor serve them. For I, the LORD your God, am a jealous God, visiting the iniquity of the fathers on the children to the third and fourth generation of those that hate me."
>
> Many people are confused about iniquities, because they do not know there is a difference between sin and iniquity. The Bible speaks of them a number of times as two different things (see Psalm 32:5: "the iniquity of my sin"). Sin is basically

the cause, and iniquity includes the effect. Generational iniquity works like this: A parent can commit a sin such as occult involvement or sexual sin—that produces a curse. The curse then causes a generational iniquity, or weakness, to pass down in the family line.

Here is an illustration: A pregnant woman has an X-ray and as a result of the radiation the unborn child becomes deformed. The baby, who did not order the X-ray, nonetheless, is affected by it and becomes a victim. Sin, like the X-ray, damages the generations to come. This is an awesome thought and should put the fear of the Lord in us before we enter into sin.

In summary, when we sin, if the sin is not repented of, any children that we have after this sin will reap what we have sown through what the Bible calls iniquity. This iniquity can come in the form of a spiritual bondage, such as different forms of addictions, or as a driving weakness for sexual sin or perversion. Generational curses can be set in motion that your children will be extremely accident prone, live a life of extreme poverty, or have chronic illnesses.

The good news is that Jesus paid the price not only for our sin but also for the iniquities of our forefathers! Iniquities do not affect our eternal salvation, but they do affect the quality of life we have on this earth. Isaiah 53:1–13 explains that He (Jesus) bore not only our sins, but our iniquities. He became a curse for us, so that we can be free!

Christ has redeemed us from the curse of the law, having become a curse for us. For it is written, "Cursed is anyone who hangs on a tree" (Galatians 3:13).[1]

A STORY BY CINDY JACOBS

In the early 1980s, my husband, Mike, and I opened our home to a woman whose husband had tried to kill her. She was about 48 years old and, other than being quite distressed over her situation (who wouldn't be), she seemed quite normal. One nice bright day this woman and I were standing in the kitchen when she suddenly grabbed her side and said, "Cindy, I hurt so bad!" Remember, at this time I was a mostly ignorant, never-had-cast-a-demon-out-of-anyone, young woman. I immediately thought things such as, *Should I call a doctor* and *Maybe you should go lie down.* She went to lie down, and I decided that I would go lay hands on her. The second I approached her, her face contorted, and a masculine voice rasped out of her female mouth, "I'm going to kill her! She deserves to die! I'm going to kill you, too!"

At that point she had my full attention!

I immediately thought of my two little children who were asleep in the other room. Something rose up inside me—that protective, mother-bear type of thing. I looked right into the eye of what I now know was a demon and boldly said, "Oh, no, you are not! You are not going to kill her or me or anyone else!"

The demonic spirit that was operating through her was trying to get off the bed. Not knowing what else to do, I grabbed my Bible and sat right on top of her. This was a rather comical scene because I was a size-four, 5-foot-2-inch individual and she was a much larger person. I recalled the conversations I had heard among students at the Christian college I had attended. Among the many ideas discussed was the principle that demons could not stand to hear about the Blood of Jesus. Having at least one weapon in my arsenal, I opened my Bible to several scriptures that address the Blood (see 1 Peter 1:2; 1 John 1:7; Hebrews 10:19).

I told the demon that it could not touch us because this woman was a blood-bought child of God and so was I. The diabolical spirit hissed, "Oh, yes I have a right to her. Her family killed Indians, murdered them and threw them down a well!"[2]

REBECCA BROWN ON GENERATIONAL INIQUITY AND CURSES

Let's look at a modern-day example. In the country of Rwanda in Africa, one tribe rose up against another and massacred thousands and thousands of people. The people of the oppressed tribe fled to camps in Zaire. There in the refugee camps thousands more died of cholera. The rest of the world watched in horror and amazement as CNN filmed the whole spectacle. Then the oppressed tribe came to power in Rwanda and began to massacre the first tribe. As a result, thousands of the people of the first tribe then fled to refugee camps in Zaire.

In February 1995, as we were flying to speak in the African nation of Ivory Coast, we were reading one of the European newspapers. A reporter who had visited the refugee camps of both tribes had written a fascinating article. When he talked to the refugees, he asked them the same question repeatedly: "Now that the war in Rwanda is ended, do you think you can go back and live in peace with the people of the other tribe?"

Without exception, the answer was the same: "No, we can never live in peace with the other tribe until the blood of our slain people has been avenged."

And so the vicious cycle continues! Wouldn't you think those people in the refugee camps would have learned by the terrible things they experienced that intertribal warfare has no benefits? But, they have not dealt with the sins of the forefathers, so they will continue to waste away in their iniquities. In satan's kingdom, blood calls for blood, and the killing never stops.

While we were ministering in Ivory Coast, we visited briefly with some Christians who had just arrived there from Liberia. They had been forced to watch as their families were massacred by another tribe. They and their families were all Christians, but they were wasting away in the iniquities of their forefathers.

The whole continent of Africa is characterized by tribal warfare. In 1995, there have been uprisings of intertribal warfare and massacres in Kenya as well. We have all seen the same things in Somalia as it was filmed by the news media. The people of Africa have never broken away from the sins of the forefathers. Each tribe is consequently ruled by particular demon gods. Demons hate people and are determined to exterminate them! Thus, the whole history of Africa has been incessant warfare and massacres among tribes. Until the Christians unite as one body and cry out to God in repentance for the sins of demon worship and hatred and warfare among their tribes as well as their ancestors' tribes, the curses from the sins of their forefathers will not be removed from their lives. Christians and non-Christians alike are being killed in those massacres. They are wasting away in the iniquities of their fathers (Leviticus 26:39).

This same problem exists here in America. The biggest problem in any large city is gang warfare and violence. Most of this is black–on–black violence. Why? Because the intertribal warfare among blacks is being carried on right here in America. Each gang is the same as a tribe. It doesn't matter that these precious people are no longer in Africa. They are still wasting away in the iniquities of their forefathers.[3]

SCRIPTURAL CURSES AND BLESSINGS

For those Bible scholars out there, there are nine curses for disobedience to God's Word (nine is the number representing judgment), and seven blessings for obedience to God's Word (seven representing perfection). They are within the writings of Deuteronomy 28–29 and Leviticus 26. The nine curses are: humiliation, barrenness or unfruitfulness, mental or physical breakdown, family breakdown, poverty or famine, defeat, oppression, failure, and God's disfavor. The seven blessings are: exaltation, health, reproductiveness, prosperity, abundance, God's favor, and victory over enemies.

One of the things listed in the Bible as a curse is that parents would not be able to enjoy their children. Oh, how many is that true for today! Another curse states that a woman would be pledged to be married and given to another. It reminds me of all the teenagers who are sleeping around today. God already knows who they are to marry, but they are being given to others. Also, in Deuteronomy 23:2 there is a curse that goes down to the tenth generation of the children that are conceived out of wedlock (illegitimacy). It states they would not enter the assembly of the Lord. I have seen this curse hinder people from getting right with God and attending church. It is oppressive, but all of these can be broken by the power of the blood of Jesus. People must realize there are consequences to their actions. In the appendix, I will list 60 sins that bring a curse in the Bible.

OPEN DOORS FROM OUR PAST OR ANCESTRY

As a Christian, and minister, I went through a betrayal that hurt me so badly that I went into a deep, dark depression. I was also suicidal. After forgiving and allowing some healing, one of my spiritual fathers prayed over me. He commanded demons of suicide (death), deep sorrow, grief, and rejection to leave me. There had been a strong oppression, but they left with violent coughing. The release was tremendous.

I have learned that traumatic experiences can open us up to demonic infiltration and attack. Satan takes advantage of any avenue he can. What an evil enemy we have.

There could be things that have opened the door for satanic bondage and the working of demons in our lives. These doors must be closed for the demons to be forced out permanently. If the legal ground is not cancelled, they will return seven times worse (Luke 11:26).

1. The Occult

The first and most deadly open door is the occult. There are three branches in the occult I will list. The intent or amount of involvement has nothing to do with it bringing a curse or not. For example, the intent may be a séance that is a joke or visiting a fortune teller because of a friend's dare. Satan doesn't care. Even if you read a horoscope one time, it seems small, but is enough to bring a curse and demonic activity. Any occult involvement brings a powerful curse on the individual, his family, and his descendants to the fourth generation. Also, powerful occult demons are loosed into the life of the individual, his family, and descendants. The occult is, and will be even more so in the future, a major open door for curses and demonic entry into someone's life. The three branches of the occult are divination, sorcery, and witchcraft.

Divination. This is the information branch of the occult. Demons of divination and familiar spirits work in this arena. Divination spirits read. For example, they can read tarot cards, palms, tea leaves, or crystal balls to make predictions. Familiar spirits are familiar with a family. That is why some psychics can know intimate things about families that no one would normally know. Psychics, clairvoyants, necromancers, or mediums all consult with and channel demons to gain information. The word divine really implies to ascertain information from the heavenlies (stars, Zodiac, planet alignment). Here are some things that could fall under this category or a similar category:

1. Fortune telling, psychics, or clairvoyance

2. Consulting the dead or séances

3. Astrology, horoscopes, astronomy, or the Zodiac

4. Meditation, yoga, chanting mantras, or astral projection

5. Psychic healings, acupuncture, or hypnosis

6. Reading tea leaves, palms, tarot cards, automatic handwriting, reading lumps on the head, crystal balls, or Ouiji boards

7. Interpreting omens

8. ESP, mind reading, mind control, prognostication, or water witching

Here is a little more about familiar spirits and spirits of divination: I personally believe that when a baby is born, God assigns an angel to watch over the individual throughout his life. Also, satan assigns a demon to be with the individual to lead them into sin, away from God, and into destruction. This demon is known as a familiar spirit. If someone gets involved in the occult, this spirit can become their spirit guide. It follows the child as it grows up. It is very familiar with the individual. Familiar spirits also travel down family bloodlines. When someone visits a fortune teller, this spirit communicates with the fortune teller to tell her what she needs to know about the person. This is how divination works. Also, spirits of divination work with occultists to read things like tarot cards and bring predictions that are usually negative. The predictions may be a future broken arm or death in the family. Demons can be released to cause these things to happen. Because the individual came to an occultist, the curse on them is legal ground to make some of these negative predictions come to pass.

Sorcery. This is the material branch of the occult. Many occultists wear certain things to bring good luck, protection, wealth, or power. Burning certain kinds of incense and using "blessed oils" from an occult store or "blessed salts" can summon demons. Certain objects can have a satanic anointing on them that will cause demons to attach to them and produce a desired effect. Here are some things that fall under this category:

1. Charms that bring good fortune or protection (luck or superstition)

2. Crystals with magic powers of some kind

3. Various jewelry that has occult symbols on it

4. Marks on the body (tattoos, body piercings, or scars from suicide attempts or self-mutilation—Leviticus 19:27-28)

5. Magic wands, daggers (athames), chalices (ritual drinking cups), altar cloths, pentagrams, or staffs of some kind

6. The occult through the media (occult TV shows, movies, or music)

7. Use of drugs to alter the state of consciousness (make more open to communication to demons), potions, certain incense, salts, oils, herbs for wiccan rituals

8. Aprons, hats, books, rings, or any material connected with Freemasonry

9. Martial arts, role-playing games (like Dungeons and Dragons)

Objects can have a satanic "anointing" on them, if I can use that word this way. This consecration toward evil causes the objects to act like a lightning rod, or magnet, that draws demons out of the atmosphere, or hell, right into people's homes! These demons are also drawn to these objects as people wear them. The demons have legal right to these objects because they belong to satan. The objects cannot be cleansed; they must be completely destroyed. If you have objects that need to be destroyed, burn them. If you cannot burn the objects, take a hammer and smash them until they are completely destroyed. After they are destroyed, remove the remains from your property.

I just prayed with a young man a few days ago who said he felt an evil presence following him around. He was a Christian, but he was wearing a "heartagram" wristband. This is an occult symbol. He did have spirits around him because of the wristband. Objects like idols, dragons, African masks, or any other objects connected with false religions will draw demons just like occult objects will. They must also be destroyed. Be very careful what you buy while in other countries!

Someone who has a tattoo or mark on the body doesn't realize what they have opened themselves up to. Witchdoctors have various tattoos for certain demons to possess them and give them certain powers. Even if the tattoo, or mark on the body, is not directly related to the occult in nature, it can still be legal ground for demons to oppress someone. If you have a tattoo or mark on the body (like the ones listed in number 4 above), simply anoint it with oil and break any work of satan associated with it. Then command any spirit that has oppressed your life to go. Applying the blood of Jesus is very powerful in cases like this. Just be led by the Spirit.

Witchcraft. This is the power branch of the occult. It can take many forms but will usually have a *priesthood* (high priest, witch doctor, shaman, or medicine man), *rituals* (performed to gain information, power, or answered prayers of participants), *sacrifices* (animal, human, or sexual), *some form of music* (often incantations from drumbeats), and some god that is worshiped and feared.

These are the four main purposes of witchcraft according to Derek Prince:[4]

1. To worship a higher spiritual being, often regarded as dangerous or malevolent

2. To control the forces of nature, such as rain or good weather for harvest

3. To ward off sickness and infertility, as in Africa, where almost every barren woman will go to a witch doctor for a potion or charm

4. To control other human beings—to terrify enemies in battle or to produce sexual desire in one person toward another

There seem to be three basic levels of witchcraft. The first would be white witchcraft. These people will call themselves white witches, wiccans, pagans, or new agers. The second level is getting into black magick. These will be those who practice blood sacrifices and rituals to call up demons to harm others. Some of these practices are voodoo, macumba, santeria, or umbanda. The last stage is hard core satanism. These people worship satan like we worship Jesus. They are violent and dangerous people. They try to present all Christians as hypocrites and say things like: "People actually believe we kill humans and breed babies!" Friend, this is exactly what they do. They say things like that to make people believe they don't. Most of America doesn't even believe in anything I have written in this chapter as any more than a fairy tale! How naive they are.

As a man or woman of God, there are those satanists that are placing curses against you. In *The Satanic Witch*, Anton Lavey taught how to make voodoo dolls and place pins in them. This can be very oppressive to the recipient of those curses. Occult curses strike suddenly and with strength.

Cindy Jacobs shares this story.

One day I was reading a book to my daughter, Mary, when I suddenly became extremely dizzy and faint. It hit with a viciousness that I knew was supernatural. I quietly said to Mary, "Honey, why don't you go play in your room for a little while?" I then called my friend, Margaret Moberly. She prayed with me and broke the curse. After that I was completely fine and the dizziness did not return.

Occult curses can cause accidents. A fall down the stairs where you feel like you were pushed, a fire that starts mysteriously, or other bizarre occurrences may be the end result of a curse. If the curse is done through a blood sacrifice, it will be stronger. Sometimes those in the occult will sacrifice a finger or a body part. At other times, they offer some other kind of sacrifice to strengthen the power of demons they send against you. Sometimes certain intersections of the city will be cursed and repeatedly accidents will take place. They need to be prayed for and the curse of accidents lifted.

At times, when a curse sent against a certain person cannot prosper, it will rebound against the sender or will affect something close to the intended victim, either in affections or proximity. I have known several instances of this. Years ago, the house across the street from Peter Wagner burned down during one of our first Spiritual Warfare Network meetings. The intercessors felt that a curse had been sent against him as we had prayed against any destruction that would come against him.

Another time, I had prayed against a spirit of death sent against a friend of mine. She was fine, but a friend of hers dropped dead in her kitchen that week. Therefore, I have learned to be sensitive to the Holy Spirit's leading to totally break the effect of the curse from prospering at all, against anyone.

Land can be cursed as well as people, and the curses will affect those who live there. We find a powerful example of healing the land in Joshua 6:26 where Joshua pronounced, "Cursed be the man before the LORD who rises up and builds this city Jericho; he shall lay its foundation with his firstborn, and with his youngest he shall set up its gates." This indeed came to pass when Hiel of Bethel rebuilt Jericho (1 Kings 16:34).[5]

Houses can be cursed and have demons in them. I always anoint with oil and pray over hotel rooms I stay in. How do I know there hasn't been homosexual activity, adulterous affairs, pornography watched, a murder take place, or witches praying in that room? I almost always feel oppression leave when I pray this way in hotel rooms.

Another attack can be while under anesthetic. It is important to have people praying for you while you are unconscious. Satan can take advantage of us being in this vulnerable condition. Some that are doctors and nurses are satanists. I am not trying to scare people; rather, I hope to make people aware. During times of unconsciousness, by either being knocked unconscious through an accident, going under anesthetic, or during hypnosis, one is very open to satanic attack and demons gaining access to their lives. The enemy will take advantage of us in our weak times.

2. Voting

I personally believe that if someone votes in leadership over a country that is pro-abortion or pro-homosexual activity, the curse these sins bring will come on them.

3. Word curses and false prayers

Another open door is words and false prayers. Words, especially from an authority figure like a father, grandfather, uncle, or pastor, are very powerful. They can rest on someone's life to bring about positive or negative results depending on the words. I don't even know how many people I have prayed over and broken negative words off them that brought a release to their lives. We have the power and authority to destroy any work of the enemy including false prayers and prayers that are not God's will. Some people might pray something stupid like, "Oh God, make the pastor very sick until he realizes the error of his ways." Demons will seize the opportunity of these words being released and try to bring about sickness in the pastor. We have the authority to lift up our voices and break negative words and false prayers!

4. Extramarital sex

Another open door is sex outside of marriage. Sex causes two to become one. There is a losing part of oneself into the partner in sex. This is all intended for marriage, because you gain back what you lost through the relationship, and God intends for the two to become one. But whether or not marriage is involved, sex will still bring the same effect. The spirits of the two engaged in intercourse open up to one another, the souls form a tie, and the bodies connect. Anything the other has in their life such as demons or satanic bondage can be imparted through sex. Can you imagine the demons at work in a prostitute's bed? A soul tie will cause someone to still fantasize about their partner at times, lust for them, dream about them, or have a feeling of being incomplete without them. This is why a married man or woman will sometimes be intimate with their spouse but fantasize about another while having sex. This can cause guilt and shame. You can take authority over these soul ties and break them.

5. Lust and pornography

Lust leading to pornography is a big one among men of God. Generational iniquity or past sins can cause a strong weakness here. You can break this. Jesus said whatever we bind and loose on the earth it will be done (Matthew 16:19; 18:18). Loosing means "destroy or untie." We have the authority in the name of Jesus to break (destroy or untie) all satanic works that are in our lives.

6. Addictions

Obviously, addictions to drugs, alcohol, or tobacco products will need to be broken. There are ministers out there that have been in ministry for years that still feel drawn strongly to these things and feel guilt and shame because of it.

7. More open doors to satan

The love of money, unforgiveness, rebellion to authority, pornography, oppressing the weak or defenseless, abortions, hate, anti-Semitism, or any prejudice can open you up to the works of satan and demons. A young man in a Teen Challenge admitted while watching a horror movie as a child he felt something enter him. He was afraid of the dark and had nightmares as a result. Fear can open us up to demons.

EIGHT STEPS I USE IN DELIVERANCE

Everyone has a different style. Mine is not any better than the next guy's, but it has worked for me. This can work for self-deliverance or with others. It can work with one person or from the pulpit with thousands. These are the steps I use:

1. *Confession and repentance* of sins, transgressions, and iniquity of oneself and ancestors (asking God to wash away sin, blot out transgression, and remove iniquity by the blood)

2. *Forgiving* all who have wronged you (as a decisive act of the will, someone could still be hurt and angry, but choose to forgive anyway)

3. *Renouncing* any occult involvement, false gods, sexual immorality, or shedding innocent blood (abortions)

4. *Pledging* one's life, family, and descendants to Christ

5. *Taking authority* over the works of satan and break them:
   - Breaking curses (nine curses listed in Bible, negative words, false prayers)
   - Breaking witchcraft curses, spells, incantations, or rituals
   - Breaking soul ties that are not of God
   - Breaking witchcraft control (mind control, caging of the mind)
   - Pulling downs strongholds in the mind, personality, emotions (soul area)
   - Destroying sickness or disease in the body
   - Breaking strongholds in relationships (strife, family division)
   - Destroying the power of pride, rebellion, or fear satan has over someone

6. *Commanding all demons* at work in someone or their family

line to be bound and cast into the abyss (where else are you going to put them) ask God to let angels help with this

7. *Replacing the works of satan with the works of Christ:*
   - Replacing curses with blessings
   - Applying the blood of Jesus everywhere the enemy has once had legal rights
   - Asking for the Holy Spirit to fill everywhere the enemy once filled

8. *Anointing marks on the body* with anointing oil, break all influence of the enemy because of them, and command any demons attached to them to leave.

This pattern of deliverance has worked so much for me. Please remember, this is only a pattern, not a rigid set of rules. Of course, not everyone needs all that is listed above, and each case is handled differently. The basic idea is to see any legal ground satan has to a person's life be cancelled (steps 1–4), the works of satan destroyed (step 5), and demons removed from the individual's life.

As I have already noted, it is vital to not leave an empty space for the enemy to fill. We must replace the works of satan with the works of Christ as seen in step 7. Sometimes a demon will manifest, and you have to cast it out first, then take care of destroying satanic works and canceling legal ground. Like I said, each case is different. We have to be led by the Spirit of God.

There are times to cast out demons in public and show the power of God. This is what Jesus always did. I can't think of one time he took a demonized person aside and cast out the demons in private. But because of something very personal, it may be wise at times to take someone to a private room and minister to them with other prayer warriors present. I always make sure someone really wants to be delivered. If they don't, you're wasting your time.

I never command demons more than one time to leave. They have to obey the first command. If they buck up against me, I look up to Jesus and say something like, "Jesus, this demon is mocking you to your face. I ask you to take care of him." It doesn't take long after that. Always have one person commanding the demons. If four or five people are yelling at it to go, the demon can sit there asking, "Which one do I have to obey?" Well, the problem is that the demon is *sitting there* asking itself which person it has to obey. This can delay a deliverance.

Don't be ashamed of the power of God publicly. The power always brings God glory and shows Christ's love for people.

A pastor friend of mine tells a story of being a young Christian and having to cast out a demon. He was walking home with his two mentors in Christianity. A woman in a park begins to manifest a demon. She began clawing a tree, and blood was going everywhere. It was a horrible sight. The demon was screaming through her that it was about to throw her in front of a bus. She took off running toward an oncoming bus. My friend yells, "Stop." The woman stops. He then casts out the demon. A cop was present who was called out because of all the noise this was causing. The cop knelt on the ground and gave his life to Jesus because of the demonstration of God's power over satan that day!

THE POWER OF GOD

1 Corinthians 4:20 states, "The kingdom of God is not a matter of talk but of power." This is so powerful. In these last days, there will be a true conflict of power. Powerless Christians will lose battles. Powerless churches will become completely ineffective. A great emphasis will once again rest on the power of God. Jesus displayed His power publicly almost every time. This display of power publicly showed His power over satan and satan's works (Acts 10:38). Also, His display of power shows His love.

Jesus could have written His name in the stars. He could have cursed a whole forest and watched it wither, only to raise it up again. He could have pointed at a mountain and moved it. He could have called down fire from heaven or preached standing on water. Why did He choose to raise the dead, cleanse lepers, heal the sick, and cast out demons? The reason is because these demonstrations of His power show His love for people. We need to seek the power of God in our lives. The power will show God's love for a hurting humanity. We also need to "earnestly" desire spiritual gifts as the Scriptures declare. These gifts are tools for success in ministry.

Be open to God while closed to satan.

I must ask, how open are you are to God's power?

What if the next revival to hit America comes through children? What if a six-year-old named Suzie goes to a thirty-three-year-old woman in Wal-Mart and says: "You are in an adulterous affair. At the age of ten, you gave your life to Jesus. He wants to know why you have run from him. He is asking you to get right with him right now." Would that be okay with you?

What if a sign that began to follow a minister was that every person he prayed for would be thrown backward and turn a 360-degree turn before hitting the ground. The minister asks Jesus, "Why are you doing this." Jesus says, "It is a sign (an act that has a message in it) that I am turning people's lives completely around." The minister goes on to say, "But Jesus, people don't like this sign. They are persecuting me for it. Even Christians are saying I am using demons to do this." Jesus replies, "Don't worry, I was persecuted because of the signs and miracles of my ministry as well. You are sharing in my sufferings." Would you be among those who persecuted this man of God? How truly open are you to a move of God?

---

1 Cindy Jacobs, *Deliver Us from Evil* (Ventura, CA: Regal Books, 2001), 211–212.

2 Jacobs, *Deliver Us from Evil,* 181–182.

3 Rebecca Brown and Daniel Yoder, *Unbroken Curses* (Clinton, AR: Wells of Joy Ministries, 1995), 31–32.

4 Derek Prince, *They Shall Expel Demons* (Grand Rapids, MI: Chosen Books), 129–130.

5 Jacobs, *Deliver Us from Evil,* 217–218.

6

Impartation: Pressing into the Last-Day Anointing

We read how the ministry was a bit much for Moses in Scripture. So the Lord spoke to him to have the 70 elders come to the tent of meeting. Numbers 11:25 says, "Then the LORD came down in the cloud and spoke with him, and he took of the Spirit that was on him and put that Spirit on the seventy elders." Also, in the story of Elijah passing his mantle onto Elisha, the prophets said, "Look the Spirit that was on Elijah is resting on Elisha" (2 Kings 2).

In the New Testament, Jesus sent out the seventy in Luke 10, and they went before him healing the sick and casting out demons under his anointing. Also, Paul told Timothy in 2 Timothy 1:6 to stir up what was in him through the laying on of Paul's hands. Paul also wrote to the church in Rome, "I long to see you that I might impart to you some spiritual gift to make you strong" (Romans 1:11).

We see here the incredible power of impartation. Like many things, satan imitates this ministry and so many throw out the good with the bad. I want to give some stories of impartation that I hope encourage you.

STORIES OF IMPARTATION

German evangelist Rinehart Bonke was a young man walking through the streets of London when he happened upon a mailbox that said,

"George Jeffreys," and he wondered, *Is this the man?*

George Jeffreys was such a powerful man of God that it is said he would walk by wheelchairs, and the chairs would tip over, knocking people out without him even touching them. The people would get up healed. When Kensington Temple reopened (George Jeffrey's old church), they found all kinds of stretchers, crutches, and braces that the sick had left behind as they left healed from the church. These items were pulled out of the basement during some cleaning.

Bonke went up to the door and asked to see Mr. Jeffreys. A house-keeper had opened the door and stated that he was in bed, old, and in bad health. She was about to say no when a voice bellowed out of the back room. "Let him in!"

Bonke met Mr. Jeffreys in the living room, and Mr. Jeffreys prayed over him. They both fell under the power as that mantle rested upon Rinehart. Now look at Rinehart Bonke's ministry today.

#

As I sat in Steve Hill's office, I was surprised that such a great man of God would take time to speak to me and be as kind as he was. We began to talk about impartation, and he referenced being prayed over by Carlos Annacondia, Benny Hinn, and Sandy Millar. An obvious impartation had taken place with these.

There is an obvious mantle that has traveled from Maria Woodworth Etter to Aimee Semple McPherson to Kathryn Kuhlman to Benny Hinn—although he does not make that claim.

There is also a mantle that has traveled from Smith Wigglesworth to Lester Summerall to Rod Parsley. I was listening to a conversation with Larry Huch and Benny Hinn. Larry felt so prompted to go to see Derek Prince before he died. Larry Huch already had a powerful deliverance ministry. He went to see Derek Prince, who laid hands on him, and impartation had taken place. This general went to be home with the Lord shortly after this encounter, but the body of Christ has benefited because of it.

#

One of the main things that has stuck out to me about the revivals of our time is the laying on of hands. When I was at Brownsville

Assembly of God in Pensacola, I received prayer as much as I could. I heard John Kilpatrick say that he had personally approved or disapproved anyone on the prayer team. He went on to say that a part of who we are is imparted from us to another through the laying on of hands, and he was very careful who lays hands on his sheep. I always appreciated that and felt very protected there. I heard an usher get up and announce that all the prayer team have badges, and no one should allow anyone without a badge to pray over them. He said that many come to the revival, and they don't know everyone. There is such wisdom in this.

A part of who someone is, and what they have, can be imparted through the laying on of hands. In 1 Timothy 5:22, Paul speaks of not being hasty in the laying on of hands and thus sharing in someone's sins. Obviously, I am careful of who I let lay hands on me, but I am also careful of who I lay my hands on. We can share in someone's sins if we are not careful in this. I anoint my hands with oil before laying them on people in altar ministry. The oil is like having a protective glove on, so to speak. It is like a buffer between you and the sin of the individual. But with oil on my hands or not, there are still some people I will not lay hands on.

IMPARTATION IN REVIVAL

There is an obvious impartation taking place in revivals in these last days. People come back with a fire in them. They have a new and fresh anointing on their lives. Truly, only the humble will allow themselves this kind of ministry. I hope to always be humble enough to let even a small child lay hands on me for impartation. I have sought out, by the leading of the Holy Spirit, certain people to pray over me that God's hand is powerfully upon them. The Lord, at one time, spoke to me that the coat of many colors is a mantle of many anointings. Without the anointing, we are ineffective in ministry. Too many are too proud to receive in this area, so they walk in less than God has for them.

A minister went to a Rodney Howard-Browne meeting. Howard-Browne was kind enough to take the time to go through and pray for everyone who wanted prayer. This man of God just stood there, stoic. Howard-Browne walked by him and touched him on the head, then walked off. The man went home. He got up to speak at his church the next Sunday. When he took the microphone, a wind blew into that place, knocking several on the floor. The minister called Howard-Browne on the phone and said, "I think something happened when you prayed for me."

#

I heard a story of a man who was so desperate and worn out in ministry he felt like getting out of the ministry. But then he went to the Brownsville Revival, where he got hands laid on him and went back home. He wasn't living in sin, but a new fire and passion was in him. If I remember the details correctly, his church grew from like 50 to about a 1,000. He had to knock out walls to house the people. Everyone in his town was getting saved. A bar owner was getting desperate because people were not coming to his bar anymore, so he invited a well-known rock band to hold a concert at his bar. He only sold ten tickets! So he and his thugs walked over to the church during a service. As he came in the back door, the pastor saw him and asked him to come forward. The pastor asked him what he wanted, and the man said he wanted to know what was going on in that church. So the pastor asked if he could pray for them. To make a long story short, the man and his thugs were hit by the power of God and ended up on the floor. The bar owner got saved, on fire for God, and went through Bible school. This is the fruit of the power of God.

A FRESH ANOINTING

In the days we are approaching, we need a fresh touch of God on our lives. Just as we should be growing in humility and love, we should be growing in power. The power of God brings God glory and shows his love to a lost world. I know of many young people who were hit by the power of God at a two-year revival God gave me. Many of them were from backgrounds that didn't accept this sort of thing, but God didn't care. Denominations are only man-made. God looks for the blood of Jesus. But I had young people tell me that they never felt God so close to them. Also, they would say that he must love them to have touched them and put them under his power on the floor. The Lord was leaning over and kissing these young people. His power showed his love for them. Many were healed, delivered (of you name it), and baptized in the Holy Spirit. There was a fresh anointing. You know that was wonderful back then, but what about now? I want a fresh anointing today. I want to be on the cutting edge of what God is doing now.

In Revelation 7:3 we see a spiritual "seal" on the foreheads of God's servants released to them. Rick Joyner said, "The best way to keep from getting satan's mark (Revelation 13:16) is to be marked by God." It is interesting that during these moves of God, servants of the Lord are laying hands on the *foreheads* of God's people. I believe this anointing that is being imparted has to do with this seal. I personally feel the anointing is what is going to distinguish God's people in these last days. Also, the wise virgins are getting extra oil for the days that are approaching (Matthew 25:1–12).

AN EVIL IMPARTATION

Just as there can be an impartation of giftings, anointings, and mantles from God, there can be an evil impartation. Now, let me say one thing at the beginning of this. I feel that many have been so afraid to receive something from the devil that they missed a move of God entirely. That is so sad. God never intended for us to live in fear. There is wisdom in being cautious, but being afraid of all supernatural power is not wisdom. I am careful about who prays for me, but I am not so afraid and closed that I won't let someone, either. I am saddened because some of my fellow ministers of deliverance have been so afraid of getting something from satan they missed God. Seek discernment. We should know when something is not of God. Some people out there have no discernment at all. So they live suspicious and critical of every move of God in some vain attempt to "protect the body." What foolishness!

Nonetheless, there are some things we must be aware of and protect ourselves from. In 1 John 4:1 we are commanded to test the spirits to see if they are of God. Also, in 1 Timothy 5:22, we are commanded to not lay hands on anyone hastily. There are reasons this is in the Bible. We obviously need to be careful about who we allow to lay hands on us, and who we lay our hands on. I want to give you some stories from a conversation with Rebecca Brown and a friend of hers who came out of satanism—a person she is calling Joyce (not her real name). Joyce is telling the stories:

"Mary (not her real name) was one of the people who trained me in how to infiltrate churches. That was her specialty. I also went to one of several special training camps for witches on how to destroy churches. It was taught by one of the well-known 'Christians' on T.V."

"Really. I'm not surprised," Rebecca said. "Paul wrote that Satan's servants would reach positions of leadership within the churches. He told the Ephesian elders that from among THEM, the church leaders, would come ravening wolves to destroy the sheep. (Acts 20:30). But tell me, what did Mary teach you?"

Joyce laughed. "I'll never forget the first time Mary commanded me to come to a certain city in Kansas where a big evangelistic crusade was being held by a particular denomination. Mary instructed me that I was to wear long sleeves, a long skirt, and had to have long hair. I had to get a hair piece because my own hair was fairly short at the time. I had never worn such sedate clothes in my life. I thought I looked terrible! Of course, my ideas about clothing have changed a lot since I started to serve Jesus."

"Anyway, I was to meet Mary at her hotel room. She knew some of the top people involved in the crusade and was there to make sure they followed their orders. When I arrived at her room, I thought I had done very well with my clothing. I had never been in a church of their denomination before. When Mary opened her door, she took one look at me and grabbed my arm. 'You come in here girl,' she snapped. 'You can't go looking like that! Remember, you must dress and act as they do or they won't accept you.' She dragged me into her bathroom and took a washcloth and proceeded to wash every scrap of make-up off my face. I was horrified. But Mary, I protested, I look terrible without makeup, I never go anywhere without at least a little.

"Mary was very impatient. 'How many times do I have to tell you that you MUST dress and act according to their expectations? If you look like them and act like them no one will question you to see if you really are a Christian or not.

"And you know, she was right. We could move freely throughout the many people at the crusade and everyone accepted us as being Christians without questioning us at all. It was during that weekend that Mary taught me more about slaying in the Spirit. Oh, I could already knock people unconscious just by touching them, but Mary told me that wasn't enough. She told me that because they were violating their own scriptures (James 5:14) by allowing anyone to lay hands on them and pray for them without even checking to see if they were a true servant of Jesus or not, that we were free to do whatever we wanted. Their God wouldn't protect them because they were in direct disobedience to His Word.

"Mary understood that when people knelt before us, or even bowed their heads before us, that they were actively submitting themselves to us and accepting whatever we wanted to give to them. Of course, they thought we were praying for them, but their submission to us gave us the legal right to put demons into them. They also directly opened the door for it by allowing their minds to go blank without testing the spirit knocking them out. Mary showed me the proper incantations to do and how to have the people hold their hands up. … Then she would tap them first on one hand then on the other, then on their forehead, making the sign of an upside down cross."

"Out they would go every time. She then did it to me and I fell over unconscious. I guess I was out for five minutes or so. When I awoke, I found that I had acquired a new demon. Mary told me this special demon would put demons into the people I prayed for. And so he did. I'm sure that isn't the only way people put demons into people by having them hold their hands like that, but that is how we did it."

Joyce continues,

"I am horrified now as I look back at the number of Christians I put demons into through that practice! They were so eager and willing to go unconscious that they accepted anything I chose to put into them. I frequently put demons of false tongues into them. Then they would wake up speaking in tongues and think they had been baptized by the Holy Spirit. … Also, those to whom I gave demons of divination, would receive all sorts of what they considered to be 'words of knowledge' from the Holy Spirit. Those words of knowledge were nothing more than information from a demon of divination. They were accurate of course. … [People] literally DEMANDED signs and miracles from the Lord. We were only too happy to give them to them. They NEVER tested any of us. If we could perform, then they decided we must be from God. …"

"You know," Joyce said, "that's where Mary was so very useful to Satan. She was willing to study the Bible to find out the place where Christians were going against God's Word. She was smart enough to know that the instant Christians were disobedient to God, we could very effectively come against them. Satan taught us that we had legal right or legal ground, as he called it, to put demons into them or afflict them with demons when they were walking in disobedience to their God."

Joyce explains how she got the "very powerful demon of divination" through "the practice whereby anyone from the congregation can come up and lay hands on, and pray with, those at the altar.

"Well, I was in just such a church that allowed that practice. They completely overlooked the scripture in James 5 that says you should have the ELDERS anoint and pray for you. There was a woman in that congregation who was a Christian. She had inherited a very powerful demon of divination. I recognized it immediately, of course. So, one day she went up to the altar for prayer. I went forward and told her and the pastor that 'god' had told me to come pray for this lady, and that she was having a problem with a demon of divination. The lady knew she was having problems, so they readily agreed with me. I laid hands on her and commanded the demon to leave her. What they did not know is that I had, with my spirit, called the demon to come into me because I wanted it. The demon promptly left her and came into me. They thought I was a really powerful Christian because the woman felt great relief as the demon left. They never knew that I was actually a witch who wanted her demon of divination! I'm sure we have no idea just how many times such things go on every day within the Christian churches."[1]

THE BALANCE OF DISCERNMENT AND WISDOM

There is a balance in this. There is a ditch on both sides of this road.

One could be overly cautious and prevent God from moving, or one could let too much go on. I don't want people to go on a witch hunt, but at the same time, we must only allow people who are tested and proven to be laying hands on the sheep. They must live holy and have the fruit of the Spirit evident in their lives. As men and women of God, we will give an account for these things one day. The days we are walking into will require great discernment and wisdom in all of this.

Remember, *satan's servants can have power and perform counterfeit miracles, but they will not have the fruit of the Spirit in their lives and live holy!* I taught on this to some young people. A Pentecostal girl came up to me and said that at a meeting, there was someone they didn't know laying hands on people, and no one questioned him. One man who fell under this man's power was taken to the hospital and was in a coma. That was obviously not God!

A FATHER'S BLESSING AND MANTLE

One thing we have been lacking in the body of Christ is fathers. We need spiritual mothers and fathers. This is why we keep reinventing the wheel. We have had to keep relearning what the previous generation knew. I believe in blessings! A father's blessing is so incredibly powerful that it will literally alter the course of someone's life. That is why biological fathers need to place blessings on their children like they did in the Bible, but also, spiritual fathers need to as well.

Every time I am around an older man or woman of God, I will interview them and let them speak into my life. I have gained valuable wisdom from this! I also ask them to pray over me. Just last week I met a general who has been on the mission field for over 42 years. Forty-two years of faithful ministry with integrity! This is a man of God. The first two years of ministry he only saw one convert, lost a baby, and almost starved to death more than once. We don't see this type of sacrifice in America. In fact, if someone was going through this in America, they would probably be persecuted. What hypocrisy! Prosperity has ruined much of the church in America.

Now, of course, this missionary has thousands of converts and churches planted all over. They have seen the dead raised, people healed of AIDS, and revival. I wanted to speak with this man of God.

He took me to his home, and I sat for at least an hour as he spoke into my life. He then laid his hands on me, prayed over me, and blessed me. What an honor. I truly cherish that time! I have had other experiences like this. I usually ask these generals what they have learned about prayer, the anointing, and any advice they have for a young minister. It is mind-boggling the wisdom that comes out of their mouths.

The first three spiritual fathers that I wanted rejected me. I say this with a right spirit, but I am glad, now, that they did. If they had mentored me, I would have turned out like them. God gave me two spiritual mothers during this time. Their names are Ruby and Addie. These are two precious elderly intercessors. They taught me how to pray, hear God's voice, and live in the power of God. I love them so much! They helped me more than they will ever know. After that, God has brought incredible men of God into my life to mentor me. I honor them. They are truly generals! They have taught me, corrected me, prayed over me, blessed me, and prayed impartation from their anointing. It has truly changed my life. I believe we need fathers and mothers in the faith. I want to teach some things I have learned about this.

Poor decisions can bring a curse and prevent a father's blessing.

As recorded in Genesis 4–5, we see that Cain's poor decisions prevented his father, Adam, from being able to bless him. Because he murdered his brother Abel, he not only missed his father's blessing but received a curse. The curse caused him to be

1. driven from the land (his life became unfruitful);

2. hidden from God's presence; and

3. a restless wanderer (his life simply driven here and there by circumstances).

God never intended this for Cain. But Cain's poor decisions caused his life to be cursed. A father's blessing will cause your life to be fruitful, God's presence to be rich in your life, and your feet to be guided into your destiny.

*Disrespecting our fathers can also
bring a curse and prevent a blessing.*

We also see in Genesis 9:18–28 that Ham disrespected his father, Noah, and inherited a curse because of it. We must honor and respect our fathers if we want their blessing.

*Not caring about our destiny can cause
someone else to get our blessing.*

Also, in Genesis 27, we see how Esau's foolishness caused him to miss his father's blessing. He sold his birthright like it was nothing. He then married Canaanite women. It was not God's will for Esau to get the blessing. Rebecca and Jacob should have prayed for God to speak to Isaac about this instead of deceiving him, but God's perfect will came about regardless. Foolishness and not caring about your destiny can cause your blessing to rest on someone else.

THE SPIRIT OF ELIJAH

We see in Malachi 4:5–6 that God is sending the Spirit of Elijah back to the church in the end times. The Bible says he will come before the great (Jesus' first coming) and dreadful (Jesus' second coming) day of the Lord. I believe when the Holy Spirit is referred to as the "Spirit of Elijah," it implies Him coming in His fullness. This is His when He comes in all seven of His attributes (Revelation 1:4; Isaiah 11:2). The Spirit of Elijah rested on John the Baptist to prepare for Christ's first coming and is resting on the Bride of Christ to prepare for his second. This revival we are in is intended to restore the hearts of the fathers back to their children, and hearts of the children back to their fathers. The Lord says, "Or else I will strike the land with a curse" (Malachi 4:6). Remember how Cain's life became unfruitful. For the father who rejects his son or the son who rejects his father, their lives will be stricken with a curse that will cause unfruitfulness in the ministry.

To illustrate this, I need to tell a story about Charles Parham and William Seymour. I derived most of this information about Seymour and Parham's lives from *God's Generals,* written by Roberts Liardon. Parham had a Pentecostal experience by being baptized in the Holy

Spirit and spoke in tongues. This was rare during this time in history. He started a Bible school and taught along these lines. Seymor was young and hungry for God. He went to the Bible school to learn. Seymour was a black man, and because of the sin of segregation, he was forced to sit in the hall and not in the classroom. But Seymour was so humble and hungry for God he didn't care.

Later, Seymour was invited to work with a home church off Bonnie Brae Street in Southern California. He met with a handful of African Americans, and they began to pray for the power of God. The Holy Spirit fell in such a powerful way that they were baptized in the Holy Spirit and spoke in tongues. Pretty soon, the crowds started coming to the house on Bonnie Brae Street. The crowds grew so large that the porch caved in. So Seymour moved the revival to an abandoned mission off of Azusa Street. This, of course, is the story of the Azusa Street Revival.

People came from all over the world to receive from the power of God. People would shake, fall, speak in tongues, prophesy, and weep in God's presence. It is said that as crowds would come in the front door, there would be a pile of bodies as the power of God overtook all of them. During this move of God, Seymour knew that most of what was going on was God, but he also knew a little was the flesh. He didn't want to quench the Holy Spirit. Being young in the ministry, he didn't feel adequate to determine what was the Spirit of God, and what was not. He was very wise to not want to quench the Spirit over a few people in the flesh here and there.

He wrote Charles Parham, asking him to come to the revival. He looked up to Parham as a spiritual father. He felt that Parham had enough ministry experience to be able to distinguish the flesh from the Spirit and help father the move of God. Parham came. No one really knows what kind of conversation took place, but Seymour padlocked Parham out of the mission. It appeared that Parham was wanting to quench what was going on. After this visit, Parham used his influence to persecute the move of God. Parham had a newsletter sent out to thousands. In the articles, he spoke very negatively about the Azusa Street Revival. The very thing God had called him to father, he was now persecuting.

Up to this point, Parham's ministry had been very fruitful. In fact, it was one of the most fruitful ministries of his time. Shortly after he persecuted and rejected Seymour, he went to Illinois. He preached at a town called Zion City. During this time, there were false accusations made of him about ungodly sexual activity. None of these things were true, but they crippled his ministry. He lost his influence, and the fruitfulness of his ministry began to die off. I personally believe this was a judgment curse because of the way he treated William Seymour. He rejected his son in the faith, and his ministry was cursed with unfruitfulness. Who knows if that revival could have extended for several more years if he had done what God wanted him to do.

Is there a son or daughter you have rejected? Is there a father or mother you have rejected? God can forgive and restore you if you ask him. It is interesting that when Elijah ascended in the fiery chariot, Elisha cried, "My father! My father!" (2 Kings 2:12). He didn't say, "My Lord, My Lord!" He knew his father in the faith and honored him. Because Elisha honored his spiritual father, he received his mantle and had a very fruitful ministry.

---

1 Rebecca Brown, *Becoming a Vessel of Honor* (New Kensington, PA: Whitaker House, 1990), 43–45.

7

Going after the High Calling: Reaching Your Full Potential as a Man or Woman of God

I want to recommend some writings by Rick Joyner that relate to this chapter. He has three books that I strongly recommend reading: *The Final Quest, The Call,* and *The Torch and the Sword.* I also recommend his book High Calling: 50 Days to a Soaring Vision. The last book I will recommend is Wanted: Extreme Christians by Steve Hill. What a powerful book! These books will change your life and ministry.

A WORD FROM STEVE HILL

All of us are responsible for living our lives in a manner that glorifies Christ and brings honor to His kingdom. As a Christian, I sense a deep responsibility to live each moment in a way that pleases my Lord. He has placed me on this planet at this time in history for a purpose. All Christians will be held accountable for what they have done with their time, talent, and treasure. We may come from different lands, different times and different cultures, but there are three things we can all be certain of: (1) one day we will all be together; (2) time, as we know it, will be no more; and (3) all our works will be judged by fire. The stark reality of this truth is what motivated the late evangelist and my dear friend Leonard Ravenhill to say, "On that day you had better hope you're not standing knee-deep in ashes."[1]

As I sat in Pastor Steve's office, he sat down in front of me in a chair. He began to speak into my life. He said, "I live every day as though it was my last."

I ask you, how do you live your life? Are you on fire for God? Do you have a passion to see souls saved? Or has the flame died down over the years of ministry?

"Do you really know the Lord?"

As I sat in the chair, speaking with Pastor Steve, the first thing he asked was if I knew Jesus. He then prodded to see if I have a relationship with him. After that, he wanted to know if I live holy. I was taken aback at first because I am a Christian and honestly wasn't expecting him to ask these questions. Man, that meeting changed my life. Of course, I know the Lord, I have a true relationship with him, and I do live holy. But the fact that he would ask me those questions inspired me.

Many times, this man of God will ask other ministers, "So what has Jesus been talking to you about?" He is trying to see if they are close to the Lord and hearing from him. I believe this is one reason that God has lifted up Steve Hill in these last days. A pastor on staff at the church (where Steve Hill was pastor) said he asked the Lord what made Pastor Steve different than other ministers. The Lord replied, "He lives holy." The staff pastor went on to say that he would watch Pastor Steve as they were out together. One time, at an airport, a half-dressed attractive woman was walking toward them. He watched as Pastor Steve turned away and looked a different direction from the woman. Pastor Steve was guarding his eyes, and his heart, from lust. He did not know the staff pastor was watching him. This type of integrity is what the Lord is looking for in his men and women.

"So I could minister and still be in hell one day!?"

Matthew 7:19–23 says, "Every tree that does not bear good fruit is cut down and thrown into the fire. Thus, by their fruit you will recognize them. Not everyone who says to me 'Lord, Lord,' will enter the kingdom of heaven, but only he who does the will of my father who is in heaven. *Many* will say to me on that day, 'Lord, Lord, did we not prophesy in your name, and in your name drive out demons and perform many miracles?' Then I will tell them plainly, 'I never knew you. Away from me, you evildoers.'"

This is one of the most sobering scriptures in the Word of God for me. Here are *many* people who knew the Lord, they were religious, and they operated in the supernatural, but ended up in hell. How could such a thing happen? I know some would say, "They were never saved to begin with." Well, you can't cast out demons unless you are saved. If you don't believe me, ask the seven sons of Sceva (Acts 19:14–16). As a matter of fact, you cannot truly prophesy or perform miracles apart from Christ. These are gifts given to believers (1 Corinthians 12).

The two complaints Jesus had about these people were that *he did not know them*, and *they were evil doers*. This is what Pastor Steve was trying to make sure I understood. He wanted to know if I have a living relationship with Jesus. Do I know him intimately? Is he speaking to me? Also do I live holy? Jesus called them evil doers. Some translations read "workers of iniquity." The Greek word there is *anomia*, which means "lawbreaker." These are people who believed they could live in sin and still make heaven their home! That is not the way this thing works, friend. I am so scared for some ministers. They get behind holy pulpits and operate in the miraculous only to go home and look at pornography. Hell will be their home if they don't repent.

So I ask you minister, do you really know Jesus? Is he speaking to you? Are you living holy? You had better make sure!

SIX SINS TO ENSURE A PLACE IN HELL

It is time for ministers to stand behind holy pulpits and point their fingers out to the crowds, saying, "You are guilty of sin, now come to the altar and get things right with God!" We need that fire again. Visitor-friendly churches and inoffensive messages are a joke. These ministers are people-pleasers, not God-pleasers! The apostle Paul prophesied about them 2,000 years ago when he wrote, "For the time will come when men will not put up with sound doctrine. Instead, to suit their own desires, they will gather unto them a great number of teachers to say what their itching ears want to hear (2 Timothy 4:3)." Friend, this is scary.

Are you a minister who is pleasing God or man? *Most of the time, you will not be able to do both.* I encourage you to do a study on sermons in the Bible. They were all bold, fiery, in your face, confrontational, and offensive. John the Baptist said, "You brood of vipers! Who warned you to flee the coming wrath? Produce fruit in keeping with repentance" (Luke 3:7–8). We will be held accountable for the message we preach. We better be telling people the truth and the whole counsel of God!

> Do you not know that the wicked will not inherit the kingdom of God? Do not be deceived: Neither the sexually immoral nor idolaters nor adulterers nor male prostitutes nor homosexual offenders nor thieves nor the greedy nor drunkards nor slanderers nor swindlers will inherit the kingdom of God. (1 Corinthians 6:9)
>
> The acts of the sinful nature are obvious: sexual immorality, impurity and debauchery, idolatry and witchcraft; hatred, discord, jealousy, fits of rage, selfish ambition, dissensions, factions and envy; drunkenness, orgies, and the like. I warn you as I did before, that those who live like this will not inherit the kingdom of God. (Galatians 5:19)
>
> "But the cowardly, the unbelieving, the vile, the murderers, the sexually immoral, those who practice magic arts, the idolaters and all liars—their place will be in the fiery lake of burning sulfur. This is the second death." (Revelation 21:8)
>
> There are six things the Lord hates, seven that are detestable [an abomination] to him: haughty eyes, a lying tongue, hands that shed innocent blood, a heart that devises wicked schemes, feet that are quick to rush into evil, a false witness who pours out lies and *a man who stirs up dissension among the brothers.* (Proverbs 6:16–19)

This is the Word of God. This is what needs to be preached to keep people out of hell. The Bible says, "My people perish because of a lack of knowledge" (Hosea 4:6). Below I list for you the six sins that will ensure someone a place in hell, whether they call themselves a

Christian or not. This nation is filled with people who call themselves Christians but don't live the life. They don't know the Lord, but think they do. This is scary.

But first, I want to say something concerning gossips who sow discord among the brethren. The Bible says it is an abomination to God. Also, in Galatians 5:19 dissension is listed as a work of the flesh that will send someone to hell. This is serious business. These people are stumbling blocks that keep churches in so much discord they can't win souls! These people are keeping others out of heaven. You can't tell me God won't judge that severely.

Here are the six sins that will ensure someone a place in hell. They are derived from the passages written above (1 Corinthians 6:9; Galatians 5:19; Revelation 21:8):

1. Worship of false gods, idolatry, occult practices

2. Sexual immorality (lust or any sexual activity outside marriage)

3. Murderers (hating others or abortions)

4. Dishonest (liars and thieves)

5. Lovers of money (greedy or covetous)

6. Drunkards (substance abusers)

PREACHING WITH CONVICTION

This type of preaching convicts people and brings them to repentance. Those who preach this are among the faithful ministers. The reason many don't is because they are afraid to offend people. Another reason is insecurity. We cannot base our security in what man thinks, but only in what Jesus thinks of us.

I want to also point out that when a woman dresses in a way that causes others to lust, she is in sin. The Bible says it would be better for her to have a millstone tied around her neck and be cast into the sea than to cause God's little ones to stumble (Matthew 18:6; Mark 9:42; Luke 17:2)! Anyone who causes young Christians to stumble will be judged very severely one day.

One of Leonard Ravenhill's famous sayings was, "If you take all the ingredients of Christianity and pour them into a funnel, what would come out the bottom is obedience." We must be faithful, obedient ministers. Let's break off any intimidation and preach with boldness and fire!

Are there people in your church on their way to hell? Steve Hill said a well-known minister of a very large church told him in private he knew many in his congregation were on their way to hell! He knew their lives outside of church.

SETTING STANDARDS

Where we set the standard of holiness, people will rise to meet that standard. If our preaching sets a low standard, that is where people will live. What a responsibility we have! I preach a very high standard of holiness. I also set a very high standard among those I allow in leadership. If they don't want to live up to that standard, they just simply won't be in leadership under my authority. We have so lowered the standard in America that it is sickening. It is time to get back to the standards of God's holy Word.

Will you be standing in a pile of ashes?

By the grace of God given to me, I laid a foundation as an expert builder, and someone else is building on it. But each one should be careful how he builds. For no one can lay any foundation other than the one already laid, which is Jesus Christ. If any man builds on this foundation using gold, silver, costly stones, wood, hay, or straw, his work will be shown for what it is, because the Day will bring it to light. It will be revealed with fire, and the fire will test the quality of each man's work. If what he has built survives, he will receive his reward. If it is burned up, he will suffer loss; he himself will be saved, but only as one escaping through the flames. (1 Corinthians 3:10–15)

What a sobering scripture! We could labor for 50 years in the ministry and have a great reputation with great accomplishments to only stand in ashes on judgment day! I believe that three things will determine whether we are standing in ashes or a mountain of jewels.

They will be obedience, complete surrender, and motives of the heart. Obedience and surrender have to do with death to self. We have got to die in Christ to be resurrected in new life.

Are there things God has asked you to do that you are not doing? Are you truly fully committed to him?

MOTIVES OF THE HEART

Ministers can flow in God's power in an awesome way. The multitudes could be healed and set free, but if they have pride in their heart, they could lose the whole reward on judgment day. Let me give you an example. God has given me some powerful moves of the Spirit. I have seen services where people had to be carried out because the power of God was so overwhelming to them. I have seen the whole congregations and leaders out under the power of God and people healed and delivered of demons. The fact of the matter is that God did this because the need is so great. He obviously did not do this because I am so great, because I am not.

We must guard our hearts. Pride of the heart will cause ashes on judgment day. Do you want God to move through you so you can be honored and receive accolades? Or do you want Jesus to be glorified? A friend of mine once said, "It is hard to stay hidden." We must know how to not exalt ourselves but remain hidden and let the Lord do the raising up if he wants to.

Another thing, if we do not minister in love, we are wasting our time. Paul says in 1 Corinthians 13 that what we do without love is done in vain. Do you really love and have compassion for those you are ministering to?

Oral Roberts tells a story of ministering one night to thousands and praying for people for a very lengthy amount of time. He was exhausted and spent. On his way out that night, a woman kept pulling at his coat and asking him for prayer. He turned in anger and gently touched her on the head. He only prayed for her so she would leave him alone. She was healed, but Oral Roberts said the Lord spoke to him and said, "I healed her, but you will not have that reward." It was like Moses, who missed the promised land because he hit the rock in anger when the Lord said to only speak to it.

I pray that Jesus helps me to see with his eyes, hear with his ears, and understand with his heart. I pray for his love and compassion for those I minister to. I ask him to help me minister in true humility and unconditional love, and to bring Him all the glory. I want to be hidden. I don't want to be standing in a pile of ashes on judgment day. The motive of the heart is a huge issue with God. Motives lead to thoughts, and thoughts lead to actions. So if the motive is wrong, eventually there will be wrong actions.

Insecurity is false humility. People that are insecure are actually very prideful. They are more concerned about what people think of them, rather than what God thinks. That is prideful. God wants us to be bold, but to make sure to give him all the glory.

One of the wisest prayers I ever prayed was that God would judge me now so that it would be easier for me on judgment day. He then began to show me all the evil in my heart. See, we will be judged as Christians at the judgment seat of Christ.

ANOTHER GOSPEL

I have heard two other gospels preached in America. This scares me. One is a gospel that "Jesus will make your life better if you come to Him." This is not in the Word! As a matter of fact, usually things get worse because satan is now battling people. This gospel has caused many to be swept into hell. Remember, we must keep the foundation the early church laid and not build on another. With this gospel, a heathen who smokes weed, sleeps around every weekend, and makes good money will say, "Cool, Jesus will make things even better for me." Well, he will then come down to the altar and ask Jesus into his life, but the motive of his heart is wrong. He needs to be convicted by the Holy Spirit and realize he is a sinner who needs a Savior. Then he needs to get the sin out of his life, if he is going to have Christ. You can't have Jesus and your sin.

The other gospel I have heard is this crazy notion that you can live in sin, play games with God, and because you call yourself a Christian, you will make heaven. America has believed this foolishness that God is overly passive and understands our sin. That is not the Word of God! Jesus said, "Repent, or you too will perish!" (Luke 13:1–9) These other gospels are powerless to change lives, because they are not the true gospel that is "the power of God unto salvation" (Romans 1:16). The true gospel is this: we are sinners who are going to hell if we don't accept the price Jesus paid for us on the cross. Then we must turn away from our sin and follow Jesus with all our hearts to the end, even if it costs us our lives. *People have to realize they are sinners and going to hell before they can truly accept Jesus' sacrifice.* Otherwise, the gospel won't make sense to them.

HELPING PEOPLE UNDERSTAND THEY ARE SINNERS

There was a sign that said, "If Jesus is the answer, what is the question?" See people don't understand they are sinners. I talk to people all the time on the streets about Jesus. Most of them will say things like, "I am a good person. God wouldn't send me to hell." So I then use the Ten Commandments to help them out.

I start asking them: "Have you ever lied or stolen anything? Have you ever looked lustfully upon a woman? Jesus said that is adultery. Have you ever hated someone from your heart? Jesus said that is murder. Have you ever wanted (coveted) what someone else had? Have you ever put something as more important in your life than God? That is an idol to you. Have you ever not been going to church the way you should be? Then you haven't kept the Sabbath. Have you ever dishonored your mom or dad? Have you ever used God's name as a cuss word? This is blasphemy and very serious."

Then I proceed to ask them, "Now that you have admitted to all these things, are you guilty or innocent of sin before God?" They will usually admit they are sinners. Then I will ask them, "Will God send you to heaven or hell?" Most will admit hell will be where they are heading. Now, I can explain to them the good news that Jesus died so their sin can be forgiven. Like soap in the natural makes you clean, Jesus' blood will wash all your sin away and make you clean before God. Now that they understand they are sinners that need a Savior, they appreciate the gospel.

The scary thing is, some of these I witness to have heard the second fake gospel I mentioned above. When I ask them if God would send them to hell they say, "If he is such a loving God, he will understand my sin." I respond by explaining to them they just broke the second of the Ten Commandments. They have used their imagination to create a false god that would send them to heaven even though they are sinners that refuse to repent.

I am blunt with people. I have people get an attitude sometimes. More times than not, people appreciate you helping them understand what true Christians believe. But those who get an attitude, I tell them, "Look, Jesus said there will be very few people in heaven. He said there is a narrow gate that leads to heaven and few find it. There is a broad gate that leads to hell and many find it. You cannot live in sin and play games with God, then expect to make heaven. The only people who will be there are those who truly know the Lord and live a holy life." They may act like they don't care, but they will think about what you said.

It is time for us to get a new baptism of fire and be as bold as lions! God wants his people to have their heads lifted up and speak with authority. We are God's servants.

COMPLETELY SOLD OUT

Are you willing to die for what you believe? I mean how committed are you? How committed are the people under your ministry? In the days we are moving into, there will be a major rise in the persecution of Christians. I sense it even as I am writing.

Michael Brown said, "You are going to see increasing opposition to the gospel message in America in the days to come because the gospel message is going to become increasingly biblical. The gospel message is going to become increasingly radical and revolutionary, and the gospel message is going to become a threat to this world's system. The gospel message is going to become an increasing threat to worldliness and materialism and greed, and the gods of sports, entertainment, and fashion. The gospel is going to become an increasing threat to the rising tide of satanism, and false religions, and the results will be the same as in the book of Acts—uproar, persecution, and a great moving of God."

Are you a martyr?

Those who have laid down their lives for the gospel inspire me! God is looking for those who want to glorify His Son in the earth. The true message of the gospel will be accompanied by great power. The Lord confirms *His Word* with signs (Mark 16:20). The Lord will raise up those who preach the cross and make room for the miraculous in their ministry.

Martyrs are first a martyr in their heart before they die in the body. What will it be like for you, if one day you are in heaven and there is a young man is sitting next to you named Titus? You ask him to tell you his story, and he says, "Sure, I had a difficult life. I grew up in Rome. My family all served Jesus. We heard of him through a man who was going door to door telling people about Jesus. One of my neighbors was healed of tuberculosis as this man prayed for him. It was a few years later that my mother was captured by the Roman guards. They poured oil on her, and I watched her be burned alive on a wooden stake because Jesus was her God.

"When my father came back home from business, he heard the news and wept bitterly. The guards came and took him away as well. I was forced to watch him be put in a coliseum, and lions ate him. The guards then took me and beat me trying to get me to renounce Jesus, but I couldn't do that! He is everything to me. I was then placed in that same coliseum the next day. I saw doors being opened on every side. Lions came out of every door. I was never so afraid in all my life. I died that day and was carried by angels to be with Jesus here. Now that I have told you my story, what is yours?"

Oh friend, we need to have a story. Not all of us have the honor of dying for the gospel in the body as a martyr, but we must have a story of totally selling out to Jesus. Sometimes it is harder to live for Jesus than to die for him. What the Lord is looking for is obedience and death to self. We must be fully committed to him in obedience to the call even if it costs us our lives. I heard a Middle Eastern woman who is a pastor's wife say she was not afraid of the terrorists because they could only kill her once. I love that.

In 1996, 160,000 people were martyred for the cause of Christ. Persecution is rising with each year. How ready are the American Christians to this kind of persecution? I would have to say many would abandon the faith if it came down to their life. The eleven disciples all gave their lives for the gospel. Andrew was killed in Greece on an X-shaped cross, feeling unworthy to die in the same way as his Lord. Bartholomew died preaching in India. He died a martyrs' death being flayed alive with knives. James the Elder was martyred first. He was slain by Herod Agrippa, having his head cut off. James the Lesser was crucified in Egypt. His body was cut into pieces. John the Revelator was spared from death by a chalice of poison someone gave him. He died of natural causes on the Isle of Patmos. Jude was shot by arrows on Mt. Ararat. Matthew became a missionary and disappeared during his labors. Peter was killed crucified upside down, because he felt unworthy to die as his Lord had died. Philip died by hanging. He requested that his body be wrapped in papyrus and not fine linen, because he was not worthy for his body to be treated as the Lord's body was. Simon the zealot died on the mission field as a martyr according to tradition. Also, according to tradition, Thomas was commissioned to build a palace for the king of India. He was killed with a spear as a martyr.

Here is another story about Andrew.

When Andrew, through his diligent preaching had brought many to the faith of Christ, Aegeas the governor asked permission of the Roman senate to force all Christians to sacrifice to and honor the Roman idols. Andrew thought he should resist Aegeas and went to him, telling him that a judge of men should first know and worship his Judge in heaven. While worshipping the true God, Andrew said, he should banish all false gods and blind idols from his mind.

Furious at Andrew, Aegeas demanded to know if he was the man who had recently overthrown the temple of the gods and persuaded men to become Christians—a "superstitious sect" that had recently been declared illegal by the Romans.

Andrew replied that the rulers of Rome didn't understand the truth. The Son of God, who came into the world for man's sake, taught that the Roman gods were devils (demons), enemies of mankind, teaching men to offend God and causing him to turn away from them. By serving the devil, men fall into all kinds of wickedness, Andrew said, and after they die, nothing but their evil deeds are remembered.

The proconsul ordered Andrew not to preach these things any more or he would face a speedy crucifixion. Whereupon Andrew replied, "I would not have preached the honor and glory of the cross if I feared the death of the cross." He was condemned to be crucified for teaching a new sect and taking away the religion of the Roman gods.

Andrew, going toward the place of execution and seeing the cross waiting for him, never changed his expression. Neither did he fail in his speech. His body fainted not, nor did his reason fail him, as often happens to men about to die. He said, "O cross, most welcomed and longed for! With a willing mind, joyfully and desirously, I come to you, being the scholar of him which did hang on you, because I have always been your lover and yearned to embrace you."[2]

This man was ready to die before the time came. Jim Eliott once said, "When it comes time for you to die, make sure that is all you have to do." Andrew was a martyr in his heart long before he saw that cross in front of him. Here was a man who fled the night Jesus was arrested. What happened to him? He had received the baptism and infilling of the Holy Spirit. A holy boldness came into his life. Notice how the Bible always says something like Peter, filled with the Holy Spirit, spoke boldly (Acts 4:8). We need a fresh baptism of fire and a boldness of the Holy Spirit in our lives to live this Christian life.

Do you know your calling?

Are you called to be an apostle, prophet, evangelist, pastor, teacher, or a combination of these? What is your function in the body? So many men and women of God are not sure. It is little wonder they aren't fulfilling what they are called to do. Very few ministers truly reach their higher purposes. Most fall very short. I have determined to not be one of those who fall short. Obviously, complete surrender and obedience to the Lord plays a huge role in this. I believe that specifically knowing what you are called to do is vital. Seek the Lord about this. Believe it or not, the Bible never says that a pastor is the one that has to lead a church. I know traditionally we see that, but other offices could lead the church. Actually, the local church is supposed to draw off all five gifts to reach full maturity and perfect unity lacking nothing (Ephesians 4:11–13). I don't know of any churches that have that. Needless to say, churches aren't reaching their highest purposes.

I heard it said it is not how you start but how you finish that counts. I am determined not to fall short of what I am called to do. I have been through some trials that have served to prepare me. So I had a slow start in ministry. This has been a grace given to me that I am thankful for. I am continuing to press on to the higher calling.

AFTER SEEING SOMEONE ACCEPT CHRIST

I personally believe if we are anointed, it is not all that difficult to lead someone to accept Christ, but it is a challenge to disciple someone. This is the highest form of teaching. Some people learn in a school setting while others learn hands on. But discipleship will be a mentoring method that can adequately teach anyone. I believe this is vital and cannot be ignored. If someone is grounded in sound doctrine of the faith, they will last. We need our roots to go down deep and be solid (Mark 4:6).

Jesus said after the *gospel of the kingdom* is preached to the whole world, the end will come. We preach the gospel of salvation, but what about the rest? We don't preach the resurrection of the dead very often. Jesus overcame death. The reason that most Christians fear death is because, deep down, they don't fully believe in the resurrection of the dead. If they did truly believe in the resurrection, in their hearts, they would not fear death. Another part of the kingdom gospel is that Jesus is returning to reign over the earth and set up his kingdom from Jerusalem. When this whole gospel of the kingdom is preached to the whole world, the end will come.

THE BLOOD, THE WATER, AND THE SPIRIT: A DEEP CONSECRATION UNTO THE LORD

1 John 5:7–8 says, "For there are three that testify: the Spirit, the water, and the blood." I feel as I close this book, I need to share something the Lord has taught me concerning this scripture.

Water baptism

I do not believe that anyone has to be water baptized to go to heaven. Like all truths, there is a ditch on both sides of the road. Some believe that you have to be water baptized to make heaven, which is ridiculous. Look at the thief on the cross who Jesus promised would be in heaven. Others pretty much neglect water baptism. I believe that water baptism is incredibly powerful and important for every believer. Jesus was not baptized only as an example to follow; there was more to it than that. Obviously, he had no sin in his life to repent of, so this was not the reason.

What a lot of people don't realize is that John the Baptist was the direct descendant of Aaron, a high priest of Israel, and should have been high priest over Israel (Luke 1:5). The reason Caiaphas was high priest was that Rome wanted him in that office. Traditionally, a high priest would pass his office to his successor through water baptism. This is why John the Baptist said, "He must increase [in prominence], but I must decrease" (John 3:30 AMP). The main reason Jesus was baptized was to receive and become the Great High Priest over all Israel.

In 1 Corinthians 10:1–5 we see the children of Israel were baptized through the Red Sea into Moses. I want you to notice the same water that baptized them *separated them from the world* (Egypt) and *killed their enemies that pursued them.* Water baptism is so powerful and should not be neglected when we are winning converts. If someone has fallen away from the Lord and returned, they should be baptized again. There is an outward spiritual cleansing of the body in water baptism (Hebrews 10:19–22; 1 Peter 3:20–22).

The power of the blood through communion

Even though water baptism is powerful, the blood saves you. We see the power of the blood in the Passover as the children of Israel were protected by the blood. The shedding of blood (which pointed to Christ) put a hedge of protection around Job, his family, and all he had (Job 1:9–10). In taking communion, there is an applying of the blood of Jesus to one's life. There have been people healed as they took communion, remembering the stripes on Jesus' back. Taking communion releases a blessing from God on the individual that partakes of it and brings the fullness of the covenant purchased at the cross. We are warned to make sure to examine ourselves when taking communion. We need to confess any sin in our lives and forgive anyone who has wronged us (rightly discerning the Lord's body—the church).

I want to bring out something powerful about taking communion. The priests of the Old Testament would eat of the sacrifices. This was a shadow of us now taking communion. When the priests would eat of the offerings, the Bible says they became so holy that what they touched became holy (Leviticus 6:18). There is a deep consecration in taking communion, and thus, applying the blood to our lives. We need to take communion often. There also seems to be a link with taking communion and having an authority figure speak a blessing. The priests of the Old Testament would cut and burn the sacrifice, then turn to the father of the family, and speak a blessing over him in the outer court.

Anointing oil

In Exodus 29 we see Aaron and his sons were washed with water, blood was sprinkled on them, and they were anointed with oil to begin their ministries. There is also a deep consecration in anointing people with oil.

As we are winning new believers, we need to see them discipled and deeply consecrated unto God. There is protection and blessing in this. Moses also clothed the priests. There can be an impartation of God's power and glory that rests on someone's life when we lay hands on them. There can also be giftings activated, anointing take place, and mantles imparted through the laying on of hands. The Lord wants us to be priests in his service. Priests have authority to consecrate a person, place, or thing as holy unto God. Let's follow through with the new believers God gives us and make sure they are adequately prepared for their newfound walk in Christ by discipling them, consecrating them, and speaking blessings over their lives.

SHOFAR WARFARE

I have found the shofar to be a powerful weapon of war! The satanic walls of Jericho came down at the shofar blast. Gideon defeated the enemy with a few men as the shofar blast threw the enemy into confusion. Jubilee is even decreed with the sounding of the shofar. I had a vision one time as I was blasting the shofar. I saw a principality holding his ears, and beneath him demons were running around in confusion and chaos!

RUN THE RACE

Many allow themselves to be intimidated by the enemy. I hear of ministers that will start to see a move of God, but when a little criticism comes out in the paper about them or a few people in the church rise up against them, they shut down the revival. These days are over. Take a look at politicians. They will endure all kinds of criticism and keep on marching straight through it. How much more should we?

Rick Joyner had a vision he records in his book The Torch and the Sword in which two old ministers were walking toward him fully armed in the armor of God, laughing together as they walked. Between them and Rick was a horde of satanic forces hissing, spitting, and doing everything they could to intimidate these old men of God. The men of God never missed a beat. They simply walked right through them as though nothing was going on. This is a sign of maturity in the Lord. Let's press through satanic attack.

Every man or woman of God who has ever done anything for the kingdom of God has come under major fire. Newspapers would slander them. Evil men and religious people would oppose them. The same is true today among those being powerfully used of God. Now when I look on the internet and see slander against a minister, my first assumption is that they must be really doing something for God!

I hope to be so much of a threat to satan that I am on his top ten hit list. I want to be known in hell like Paul (Acts 19:15). I would be honored to have my name beside these who are being persecuted because of the power of God and the fruit of ministry they are seeing. I know one thing, I have made up my mind that I am going after God. Come hell or high water, a Jezebel spirit, black magic witches or warlocks, I am going after God. I will not be intimidated or fall short. I hope that passion is in all of us in these last days.

Let's run the race as to win. Keep going after God with all your heart! Don't ever stop going after God. Stay on fire for Jesus and go after souls. I hope this book has challenged you. It has been a challenge to write. I have prayed and fasted for those who would read this book. I believe it is a divine appointment that you are reading it. Now let me speak this blessing over you:

May God bless you, keep you, and protect you
May He make his face to shine upon you
And lift up his countenance toward you
And give you his peace
May your ministry be fruitful
I speak that the Lord bless you to reach your highest purposes
May you reach your full potential in all things
And maximum level of fruitfulness in the ministry
May you fulfill all God has called you to do
I bless you now in the mighty name of Jesus

1 Steve Hill, *Extreme Christians Wanted* (Gospel Light, 2002), 3.
2 John Bevere, *Breaking Intimidation* (Lake Mary, FL: Charisma House, 1995), epilogue.

Appendix 1

Blessings to Speak[1]

PARENTAL BLESSING

(To be spoken over children)

May the Lord bless you with

The Blessings given to Abraham and every spiritual blessing in Christ

May every promise of God be yours

The Lord bless you with exaltation and promotion

Ability, creativity

The power to gain wealth

Prosperity and abundance

A healthy and long life

Reproductiveness and healthy children

Favor with God and favor with man

Victory over enemies

Angelic protection and supernatural intervention to protect

Assurance of God's love and grace

Clear direction and leading of the Holy Spirit in all things

Controlled and disciplined life

Courage, faith

Spiritual perception of God's truths

Happiness, Fulfillment, Contentment, Hope, and Peace
A good outlook on life, and a listening ear to God
An obedient heart to God's Spirit and his word
A pleasant personality, pleasant speech, protection, provision
Safety, strength, success, trust, wisdom
A godly, virtuous, and gracious spouse; a blessed marriage; and
Blessed healthy children who love and serve Christ

May you enjoy your children and they be a joy to you

May the works of your hands be blessed

May goodness and mercy follow you all your days; and

May you dwell in the house of the Lord forever

CONGREGATIONAL BLESSING

(From a pastor over his church)
In the name of Jesus Christ, the Lord bless you with the blessings given to Abraham, every spiritual blessing in Christ and the promises of God, which are yes and amen.

The Holy Spirit make you healthy and strong in body, mind, and spirit to move in faith and expectancy.

God's angels be with you to protect and keep you.

Be blessed with supernatural strength to turn your eyes from foolish, worthless, and evil things; instead may you behold the beauty of the things that God has planned for you as you obey His Word.

I bless your ears to hear the lovely and uplifting and encouraging and to shut out the demeaning and negative,

Your feet to walk in holiness and your steps to be ordered of the Lord, and

Your hands to be tender helping hands to those in need, hands that bless.

The Lord bless you with a humble and teachable spirit and your hearts to be humble and receptive to one another and to the things of God and not the world and

Your mind to be strong, disciplined, balanced and faith filled.

God's grace be upon your home that it may be a sanctuary of rest and renewal. A haven of peace where sounds of joy and laughter grace its walls. Where love and unconditional acceptance of one another is consistent.

God give you success and prosperity in your business and places of labor as you obey the Bible concerning the tithes and offerings.

God give you spiritual strength to overcome the evil one and avoid temptation, overcome satan's deceptions, and the accuser of the brethren in all things.

God's grace be upon you to fulfill your dreams and visions.

May goodness and mercy follow you all the days of your long life.

The Lord bless you with an ever-increasing, perpetual revival. May your heart be ablaze white hot in love with Jesus, and He be your everything. May you have a passion and hunger and thirst for the things of God, and a godly hatred for what is evil.

Therefore, in your lying down and in your rising, your going out and coming in, whether in the city or in the country, the Lord bless you and keep and protect you from any harm coming near you. The Lord continually make His face shine upon you and be gracious unto you. The Lord lift up His countenance upon you and give you his rest and peace.

I BLESS YOU IN JESUS' NAME.

DEPARTURE BLESSING

(Sending someone with your blessing)
As you return from where God has brought you, may the Lord bless

you to live a godly Christian life.

The Lord bless you with a hunger and thirst for righteousness and a godly hatred for the things of the world, the flesh, and the devil.

The Lord supernaturally protect you by a hedge of protection, a wall of fire, a shielding of God's power, and angels encamping round about you, your family, and dwelling from this day forward—and in the same way, may God's glory be your defense.

May you continue in your first love and your passion for Christ grow and the Lord cause your prayer life to be rich and powerful.

The Lord grant you depth and revelation out of his Word.

May discipline to read the word and pray consistently be yours.

The Lord grant you an ever-increasing perpetual revival in Jesus' name.

The Lord go before you and make your way smooth. May satan's plans for your life be cancelled and the plans of God be firmly established.

May relationships that are not of God be removed and blocked from coming into your life. The Lord provide you with a church home and family. May you be given godly Christian friends that will be a strength to you and your character.

Righteous judgement and wisdom in all things be yours.

The Lord make you strong in him and his mighty power. Be more than a conqueror, an overcomer, led in triumphal procession, and may you walk in the fullness of the freedom and victory purchased for you at the cross.

The Lord give you supernatural strength to overcome temptation, any deception of the enemy, and the accuser of the brethren in all things.

The fragrance of the knowledge of Christ spread through you wherever you go, and the Lord give you the grace to be the bold witness God desires you to be for him.

May the Spirit of God be upon you in power from this day forward to guide, empower, strengthen, protect, and fill you daily.

May you apply all that you have learned in the Lord, and He be your strength, shield, and great reward.

The blessings given to Abraham and every spiritual blessing in Christ be yours.

The promises of God, which are yes and amen, be yours.

The Lord bless and keep you in all your ways. May he cause his face to always shine upon you, and He be gracious unto you. May he give you continual rest and peace. I bless you now in Jesus' name.

MINISTERIAL BLESSING

(To speak over a spiritual son or daughter)
The Lord, the God of Israel, bless you abundantly. May you be blessed in your going out and your coming in, at all times, whether in the city or the country. May blessings upon blessings shower down upon you, your ministry, and works of your hands like continual showers of rain.

May you be protected from your enemies and all who would seek to do you harm.

The Lord make your enemies your footstool, cause you to possess the gates of your enemies, make the enemies that come at you in one direction flee before you in seven, and make your enemies fall by the sword before you.

The Lord cause his face to shine upon you, look upon you with his favor, make your life and ministry fruitful, and greatly bless the works of your hands. The Lord be gracious unto you, lift up his countenance toward you, and give you his peace.

May all you set your hands to do prosper before you, and everywhere the soles of your feet tread be given unto you.

May you tread upon snakes and scorpions, overcome all the power of the enemy, and nothing harm you.

The Lord encamp His angels round about you and protect you on every side. May His warring angels fight with you and on your behalf. May you be given rest, and the Lord grant you His peace.

The Lord bless your ministry to facilitate the last day move of His Spirit, and the Lord keep you in a continual flow of what He is doing.

May the Lord supernaturally bless your ministry to be successful, fruitful, and productive.

May many souls from the four corners of the earth come to know Christ and be discipled through your life and ministry.

The Lord use you to disciple the nations and help fulfill the great commission.

The healing power of God flow through you in Jesus' name. May the brokenhearted be bound up, the lame walk, the mute speak, and the blind see. Let miracles and healings follow your ministry.

May the Lord use you to set the oppressed free, and deliverance follow your ministry, and Satan's works be replaced by the works of Christ through you.

Let revival flow through you and your ministry to the ends of the earth. May the river of God flow through you, His winds blow, His fire consume, and His rain saturate those whom God sends you to. May many be baptized in the Holy Spirit and fire through you.

May depth of insight be yours. The Lord bless you with the Spirit of wisdom and revelation into the mysteries and secrets of life. May the eyes of your heart be flooded with the light of God's truth to know and understand the hope to which he has called you and the riches of his glorious inheritance he has for his saints.

May your study time always prepare you to teach and instruct the lambs and sheep of God. To preach the gospel of good tidings to the meek, the poor and the afflicted, to bind up and heal the brokenhearted and set the captives free. May the Spirit of God be upon you in power in all you do for Christ.

The Lord bless your wife to be virtuous and gracious in every way, for a godly woman wins honor and is a crowning joy to her husband.

May you love and enjoy your children. The Lord bless your family with a calm undisturbed heart and mind, for they are the health and life of the body.

The Lord grant you out of the rich treasure of his glory, to be strengthened and reinforced with mighty power in your inner man by the Holy Spirit indwelling your innermost being and personality.

May the Lord bless you and your ministry abundantly and through you be a blessing to the nations- even to the ends of the earth.

I bless you and your ministry now in Jesus' name!

---

1 Tremendously influenced by teachings of John Kilpatrick.

Appendix 2

Sixty Sins That Bring a Curse

1. Cursing or mistreating Jews (Genesis12:3; Numbers 24:9)

2. Willing deception (Joshua 9:22-23; Jeremiah 48:10; Genesis 27:12)

3. Adulterous women (Numbers 5:27)

4. Disobedience to the Lord's commandments (Deuteronomy 11:28; Daniel 9:11; Jeremiah 11:3)

5. Idolatry (Jeremiah 44:8; Deuteronomy 5:8-9; 29:18-20; Exodus 20:5)

6. Keeping or owning cursed objects (Deuteronomy 7:25; Joshua 6:18)

7. Refusing to come to the Lord's help (Judges 5:23)

8. The house of the wicked (Proverbs 3:33)

9. Refusing to give to the poor (Proverbs 28:27)

10. The earth, because of man's disobedience (Isaiah 24:3-6)

11. Jerusalem is a curse to all nations if Jews rebel against God (Jeremiah 26:4-6)

12. Thievery and swearing falsely by the Lord's name (Zechariah 5:4)

13. Ministers failing to give the glory to God (Malachi 2:1-2)

14. Robbing God of tithes and offerings (Malachi 3:8-9)

15. Hearkening unto their wives instead of God (Genesis3:17)

16. Dishonoring one's parents (Deuteronomy 27:16)

17. Creating graven images (Deuteronomy 27:15)

18. Willfully cheating people out of their properties (Deuteronomy 27:17)

19. Taking advantage of blind people (Deuteronomy 27:18)

20. Oppressing strangers, widows, or the fatherless (Deuteronomy 27:19; Exodus 22:22–24)

21. Lying with one's father's wife (Deuteronomy 27:20)

22. Lying with any animal (Deuteronomy 27:21; Exodus 22:19)

23. Lying with one's sister (incest) (Deuteronomy 27:22)

24. Smiting one's neighbors secretly (Deuteronomy 27:24)

26. Adultery (Deuteronomy 22:22–27; Job 24:15–18)

27. Pride (Psalm 119:21)

28. Trusting in man (or the flesh) and not in the Lord (Jeremiah 17:5)

29. Doing the work of the Lord deceitfully (Jeremiah 48:10)

30. Keeping back the sword from blood (Jeremiah 48:10; 1 Kings 20:35–42)

31. Rewarding evil for good (Proverbs 17:13)

32. Conceiving illegitimate children (for ten generations) (Deuteronomy 23:2)

33. Murder (Exodus 21:12)

34. Deliberate murder (Exodus 21:14)

35. Children striking their parents (Exodus 21:15)

36. Kidnapping (Exodus 21:16; Deuteronomy 24:7)

37. Cursing one's parents (Exodus 21:17)

38. Causing the unborn to die (Exodus 21:22–23)

39. Not preventing death (Exodus 21:29)

40. Practicing witchcraft (Exodus 22:18)

41. Sacrifice (worship) to false gods (Exodus 22:20)

42. Attempting to turn anyone away from the Lord (Deuteronomy 13:6–18)

43. Following horoscopes (astrology) (Deuteronomy 17:2–5)

44. Rebelling against pastors and leaders (Deuteronomy 17:12)

45. Prophesying falsely (Deuteronomy 18:19–22)

46. Women not keeping their virginity until married (Deuteronomy 22:13–21)

47. Parents not disciplining their children, but honoring them above God (1 Samuel 2:27–36)

48. Cursing one's rulers (Exodus 22:28; 1 Kings 2:8–9)

49. Teaching rebellion against the Lord (Jeremiah 28:16–17)

50. Refusing to warn sinners (Ezekiel 3:18–21)

51. Defiling the Sabbath (Exodus 31:14; Numbers 15:32–36)

52. Sacrificing human beings (Leviticus 20:2)

53. Participating in seances and fortunetelling (Leviticus 20:6)

54. Involvement in homosexual and lesbian relationships (Leviticus 20:13)

55. Necromancy (consulting the dead) and fortune tellers (Leviticus 20:27)

56. Blasphemy of the Lord's name (Leviticus 24:15–16)

57. Being carnally minded (Romans 8:6)

58. Sodomy (Genesis19:5–15, 24–25)

59. Children rebelling (Deuteronomy 21:18–21)

60. Tolerating a Jezebel spirit (Revelation 2:20–23)

The Sixty Sins that Bring a Curse inspired and partially taken from Richard Ing's book *Spiritual Warfare.*